THE MAN-EATER OF PUNANAI

THE MAN-EATER OF PUNANAI

A journey of discovery to the jungles of old Ceylon

Christopher Ondaatje [signature]

Christopher Ondaatje

Juliana + John

Wonderful to see you in
Bermuda ——— a long way from
old Ceylon (and old Montreal).
Please come back again soon —
and call us ——— 292-1555.
Great lunch!
Christopher
Apl. 1992

HarperCollinsPublishersLtd

A SATURDAY NIGHT BOOK

First Edition

Canadian Cataloguing in Publication Data

Ondaatje, Christopher
            The man-eater of Punanai

ISBN 0-00-215747-0

1. Ondaatje, Christopher — Journeys — Sri Lanka — Punanai.
2. Punanai (Sri Lanka) — Description. 3. Punanai (Sri Lanka) — Social life and customs.
4. Ondaatje, Christopher. I. Title.

DS490.P805   1992   954.93   C91-095706-1

92 93 94 95 96   ML   5 4 3 2 1

Book design by Jackie Young/ink.
Printing and Binding by Metropole Litho, Quebec, Canada.
Film Separations by Ultragraphics, Dublin, Ireland.
Project Management by Paula Chabanais & Associates.

Distributed in Sri Lanka by Studio Times Limited, 16/1 Skelton Road, Colombo 5, Sri Lanka.

Printed and Bound in Canada.

For my father
Philip Mervyn Ondaatje

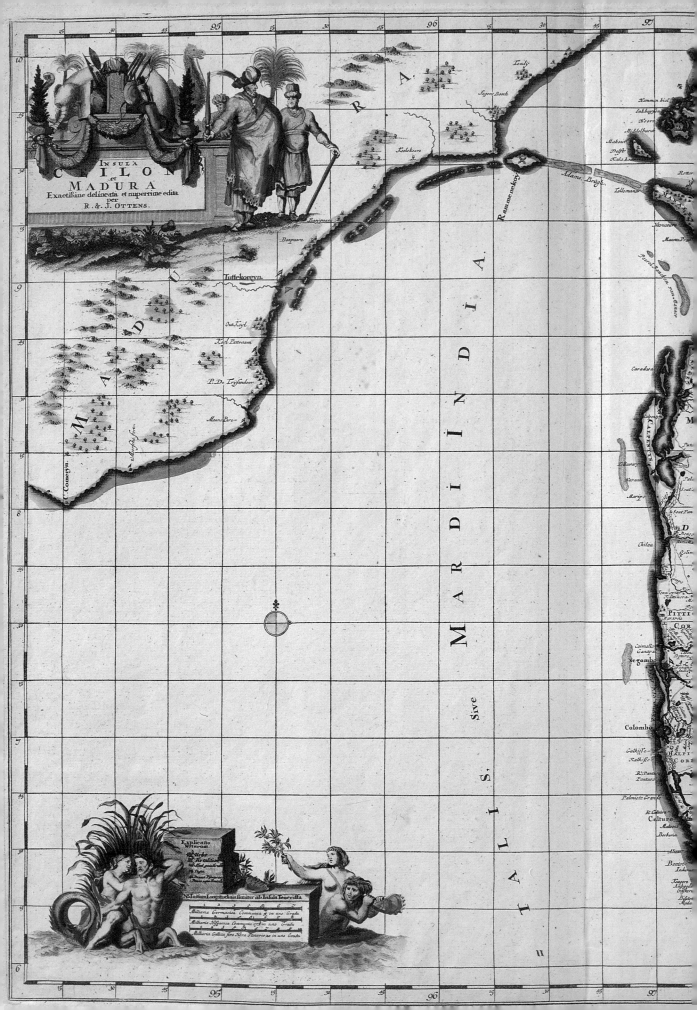

INSULA
CEILON
et
MADURA
Exactissime delineata, et nuperrime edita
per
R. & J. OTTENS.

M A D U R A

C. Comeryn

Tuttekoreyn.

Manna Bare

P. D. Tryfundoor

Keel Pattanam

Out Keyl

Banpaare

Bavipaan

Koolaksore

Ramanenkoyl

Adams Brugh

Tellemanse

Sagens Bosch

Taalÿ

M A R D I   I N D I A.

Sive

M A R I   T A L I S,

Carada

Chilau

Calpenten   CALPENTYN

Negombo

Colombo

Galkisse

Rathisse

Palmietz Grande

Ceiture

Berberin

Beutot
Indurure

Explicatio Literarum

NB Initium Longitudinis sumitur ab Insula Teneriffa.

Milliaria Germanica Communia 15 in uno Gradu
Milliaria Hispanica Communia 17½ in uno Gradu
Milliaria Gallica fere Hora Panerise 20 in uno Gradu

II

Contents

Insula Ceilon et Madura
R. & J. Ottens, Amsterdam, 1740

Acknowledgements

I could not have written this book without the help of my sister Gillian Ratnayake. She persisted in her efforts to get me to return to Sri Lanka and convinced me that the visit would enable me to bury my ghosts once and for all. I am grateful for her wonderful understanding and patience and for her energetic assistance in organizing my strange and sometimes rather perilous journey.

Childers Jayawardhana, Lucky Senatilleke, and Mahinda "Raja" Rajapakse travelled with me everywhere and greatly enriched the expedition - and my experience of Sri Lanka.

I have talked a lot about Nihal Fernando in this book. For his friendship, moral support, extensive knowledge and experience, and practical assistance I am immensely grateful.

Nirmala de Mel, too, deserves thanks for her patience and encouragement and for her skill in solving a number of difficult organizational problems.

Much of the text of this book was written on the run - in the jungles, in a jeep, whenever I could snatch a moment. For expert editorial guidance in the task of structuring the narrative, my sincere thanks go to Ron Graham. Margaret Allen helped to prepare the final manuscript for publication.

Finally, I am indebted to His Excellency Walter Rupesinghe, the high commissioner for Sri Lanka in Canada. His sensitivity, expertise, and good advice enabled me to eliminate many inaccuracies from the final manuscript.

Introduction

"This is my Father's world," an old Anglican hymn goes, "And to my listening ears, All nature sings, and round me rings, The music of the spheres." It is the kind of hymn much deployed in boys' schools of the type Christopher Ondaatje ended up attending in England after his father dispatched him from an idyllic childhood on the wild and sunlit uplands of old Ceylon. It was, apparently, a time for manners to be polished, for sensitivities to be tamed, and for "the music of the spheres" to be constrained within grey chapel walls. It was also, I suspect, the first time Ondaatje tried to come to some preliminary terms with the often overwhelming presence of his father.

Brooding about a sire is a lifetime's occupation and not always an easy one, for much goes on between fathers and sons that is never spoken and only rarely hinted at. Yet how these fragments of early memory haunt us, especially when it comes time for us to enact the same roles. Whether our fathers were famous men and bold, or reclusive and gentle, their spectres looming up from remembered boyhood motivate so much more than we ever care or dare to acknowledge that any sort of sudden confrontation can be jolting. And also reaffirming. When Christopher Ondaatje confronts head-on his father's troubling legacy in Sri Lanka, the drama rivals that provided by any of the attendant cast –Tamil Tiger terrorists and the beasts of the jungle included. This is a remarkable account of a journey into the past and the present. It is also an act of stark confrontation: wilful, alarming, and poignant.

In Canada, his adopted home, Christopher Ondaatje is an officially controversial person, much served up in the media and sometimes dressed down. I think of "controversial" in its widest possible sense. He elicits both admiration and anger, depending on what he is up to – his unpredictability being as fascinating to journalists as his great success. Here, for example, are things I had heard about Ondaatje before I ever met him, things that are left in the jumble of their evident contradictions: he has made and lost fortunes; in business, he is a gambler of great daring who can also cut out of the game faster than one of his beloved leopards at full run; he is remarkably considerate and passionate but can be as cold-blooded about obtaining or abandoning goals; he is a generous benefactor, a hard bargainer, and an altruistic dreamer; he is fickle and a pushover for a wild and chancy scheme that captures his imagination. He is a man of immense sensibility and charm.

Who then is the real Christopher Ondaatje? I learned more about him from reading the galleys of *The Man-Eater of Punanai* than from dozens of conversations we've shared or anything I ever read about him. And what I learned was this: his fullest measure can be taken by his obsessive curiosity and his desire to track down the seemingly unobtainable. This is a man who is ruled by a life force or assertiveness that has him lusting for challenge and the unknown. He has a large capacity for adventure, loves to spring surprises, and his enthusiasms constantly threaten to overwhelm his capacity to contain them. Do I ever want to go with Ondaatje into the jungles of Sri Lanka or to the deserts of the Kalahari? No thanks, he would exhaust me and I would disappoint him. Would I want him at my side in a tight moment of danger, or would I wrangle with him in a pub on politics or religion or the history of human cupidity? Any old time, anywhere.

Most of all, though, I feel beguiled by his complicated passion to reach out and understand. Coming to terms with the sad and terrible conclusion of his father's life, when the family fortunes took a calamitous tumble, he struggles in this book to fix in his mind the failure of character that hounded a proud and sensitive man into spiralling self-destruction. In adversity, after all, comes the measure of our ability to survive. In the adversity of their fathers, sons try to find either inspiration or cautionary insight:

> Though he [my father] could be kind and lenient to a fault, he could also be a tyrant. Though he could be very loving, he always expected things to be done his way. And though he could be vulnerable, he sometimes reduced everything to rubble with his thoughtlessness, his drunkenness, his borrowing, and his irresponsibility towards his business and, sometimes, his family. At root, I suspect that, despite his very attractive qualities and his aristocratic demeanour, he lacked self-esteem. This lack perhaps stemmed from the awe in which he held my grandfather, and also perhaps from being the only Ceylonese among Carson's Scottish and English tea agents. Despite his initial competence as a manager, he never

felt he fulfilled the expectations of either, and when the appearance of moderate success collapsed, he had no inner confidence to fall back on.

[He] was happiest doing the simplest things: being with his family, running the estate, discussing the books he was reading, teaching his children, talking to people. Somehow he thought he had to aim higher in order to be happy. He didn't have to. He shouldn't have tried to. But "the devil drives," and it drove him to his sad end. And his sad end drove me because of my own frustration and loss.

Not all fathers and their deeds drive their sons to go as deeply and painfully into the past as this. Not all sons have the courage to embark on such a passage. More than the lore of a famous leopard was being sought in the jungles of old Ceylon when Christopher Ondaatje got tired of business in Toronto and went on his adventure. More was sought, and more was found.

JOHN FRASER
Editor, *Saturday Night*
Toronto

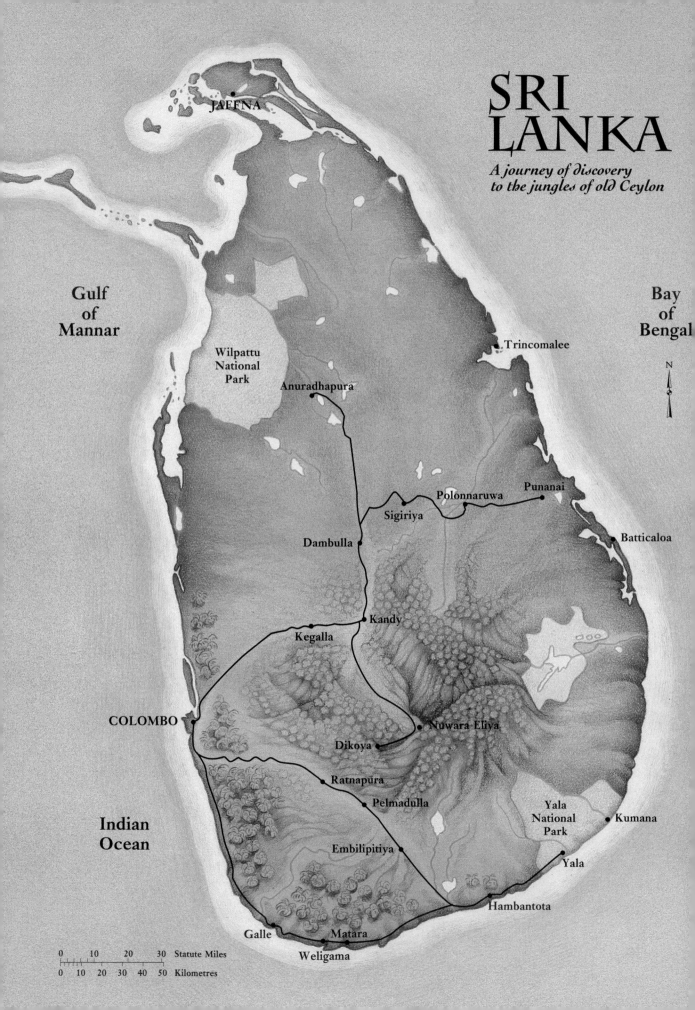

SRI LANKA

A journey of discovery
to the jungles of old Ceylon

Gulf
of
Mannar

Bay
of
Bengal

N

JAFFNA

Trincomalee

Wilpattu
National
Park

Anuradhapura

Punanai

Polonnaruwa

Sigiriya

Batticaloa

Dambulla

Kandy

Kegalla

COLOMBO

Nuwara Eliya

Dikoya

Ratnapura

Pelmadulla

Yala
National
Park

Kumana

Indian
Ocean

Embilipitiya

Yala

Hambantota

Galle

Matara

Weligama

0   10   20   30   Statute Miles

0 10 20 30 40 50   Kilometres

"It was a strange world, a world of bare and brutal facts, of superstition, of grotesque imagination; a world of trees and the perpetual twilight of their shade; a world of hunger and fear and devils, where a man was helpless before the unseen and unintelligible powers surrounding him."

LEONARD WOOLF, **The Village in the Jungle**

1
Prologue

I was huddling behind a locked door of a bathroom, leaning against a stone wall, waiting tensely for the next unnerving noise. It was after two o'clock in the morning. I was alone and far from home: in fact, on the other side of the world. I was in a room at the end of the corridor, away from the others. My body was damp with heat and anxiety. I pressed it against the wall, which felt cool and safe, and I listened intently.

The hum of the fan. Mosquitoes. Voices whispering outside my window. Steps on the gravel driveway. Military jeeps coming and going. A dog's high-pitched bark. An order was barked out too in a strange tongue – the language of my forefathers, the sound of my childhood.

I was on the edge of a jungle in the land of my ancestors, the country of my childhood – Ceylon then, Sri Lanka now, Serendib once upon a time. In the darkness, fear and uncertainty crowded around me. Outside the bungalow predators lurked – the wild animals of the jungle, the terrorists who were rumoured to be in the area, the five armed soldiers in the grounds. I was a stranger here and therefore a target for unwanted attention. I worried that someone might try to break into my room. That's why I had locked myself in this damp stone bathroom with the vague menace of the night all around me.

In my heightened state of tension that night, even the memories crowding in on me seemed threatening. Now that I am back in Canada, in cold daylight, surrounded by all my things, all the trappings of security, it is impossible for me really to understand that fear. I can hardly recognize the person huddling against the stone wall, with the cold, damp cement floor beneath his bare feet, sweating in the humidity of the tropical night.

On the shelves in my library are several red, leather-bound volumes that contain a multitude of clippings and reports, a whole career – of fantasy, of exaggeration, but also of achievement. I am barely able to tolerate the thought of it anymore. The clippings record the life of a different person, a different journey, a different career. It is true that I laboured hard and long to put it all together, but now a lot of it – the corporations, the personalities, the successes, the failures, the empire building, the power, the money – seems like nonsense: no more than a row of red, leather-bound volumes sitting neatly on my library shelf. They are of no real importance. Not now anyway.

What is important? The answers may have something to do with the thin, tired man leaning against the cold stone wall at the edge of the jungles of Sri Lanka. The myth is not the man. This is a real situation bound by surprise and fear. The answer to the question lies in the discovery.

When I was a boy in Ceylon, as Sri Lanka was known until 1972, my father took me on a trip around the island. It was probably the highlight of my life up until then, and it was certainly the last thing we did alone together. The year was 1946, I was twelve, our lives were about to change dramatically, and we would be separated forever. For me the change meant school in England, a financial career in London, and the makings of a considerable success in Canada. For him it meant disgrace, drink, and death.

Our final journey together took us by car and driver from my father's tea estate in the Kandyan foothills first down to the Yala Game Reserve on the southeast coast and then north to the ancient cities of Sigiriya, Anuradhapura, and Polonnaruwa. More than any other members of the family, my father and I shared a love of the outdoors and of wildlife; it was a great bond that he had encouraged between us on our walks around the estate or on holidays.

"Christopher, do you want to come?" he used to yell as he set off on his inspections, and I always went, partly because I loved him so much and partly because he would be angry if I didn't go. As we walked, he taught me about history, about nature, about confidence, and he always encouraged me in any interest I had, whether it was in birds or athletics or boating.

Of the fortnight or so we enjoyed together on our drive around the island in 1946, I particularly loved our days and nights at the Ruhuna National Park, more commonly called Yala. It was there at that time that I saw my first leopard. There were leopards in the hills near our tea estate, but I had never seen them. This time, however, as we were driving through the jungle – so called in Ceylon, but more a dry wilderness of thorn bushes and scrub than a rain

A Colombo schoolboy returning home in the late afternoon. Sri Lanka has one of the highest rates of literacy in the world.

forest – I caught a brief glimpse of a leopard. It excited me terribly and whetted my appetite for more, and when we returned to our bungalow for dinner I was full of questions for the trackers: how dangerous are leopards, what are their habits, do they eat people? Though I forgot most of what I was told, only learning it again much later, I never forgot the guides' story of the man-eater of Punanai.*

Over the course of a year or two in the early 1920s, an exceptionally dangerous and audacious leopard had killed and devoured at least twenty human beings in the region of Punanai, keeping the tiny village in terror. Villagers disappeared from their mud huts in the night. Coolies vanished as they worked on the railway lines. Bearers walking empty stretches of the road to Batticaloa were ambushed and eaten. Children were stolen in broad daylight. Such was the leopard's fearlessness and cunning that the local inhabitants became afraid to go to work, and travellers were warned to avoid the area unless armed and in a group. The state of panic persisted until an English tea planter and sportsman, Captain Shelton Agar, finally shot the man-eater in 1924.

The legend, told at sunset in pidgin English and in horrifying detail, frightened me, an impressionable twelve-year-old, out of my wits. Yala was very wild then, and I thought that Punanai was close by. The bungalow was remote yet dangerously exposed, there was only the light of the kerosene lamps, and I had a vivid imagination. Not that it took much imagination, as I lay on a cot on the veranda in the hot night, to fear a leopard moving in the dark bush just beyond the parapet. As usual, the night was still and black – deeply still, deeply black – but with the silence periodically shattered by jungle sounds: the chattering of monkeys, the shriek of peacocks, the bark of deer, the call of countless birds, and sometimes the guttural sawing noise of a leopard. If the sounds were isolated, they didn't matter. But if they grew into a commotion of monkeys and birds and deer, then something was happening out there. I couldn't help but be awake, I couldn't help but listen hour after hour for the next outbreak of sounds. If it happened farther away, the danger was moving away. If it erupted nearby, the danger was moving in. What was it? A leopard? It was coming closer and closer. Then it's here, by my foot, though not really at all.

---

* *Punanai is a little village in northeast Sri Lanka on the trunk road and railway from Colombo to Batticaloa.*

In some ways, I suppose, the man I am today is closer to my twelve-year-old self than to the driven financier I have been for much of my working life. I enjoy the game of business enormously, but for a while it was all-consuming. The trick of success is to be single-minded. You have to put all your ability and concentration into what you want to achieve. I could never relax, I was never free, I was in essence a slave to what I had created. Rarely could I get away for a holiday, and if I did, I was always on the telephone. As the profits grew, the obligations and the pressures also grew, until I felt I was being strangled or drowned by a monster. Finally, in 1988, I had had enough. I began to liberate myself from deals and telephones.

The first step in the process was a journey to East Africa, from which emerged my book *Leopard in the Afternoon*. It was a liberation of my time, of my intellect, and of all the possibilities now open to my remaining years. It also ignited in me a fervour to return to Sri Lanka. In Nairobi I saw scenes and smelt smells that brought back memories of Colombo. In the Serengeti I knew again the joy of the outdoors and the thrill of the wildlife I had known as a boy in Yala. More strangely, perhaps, from the start of the safari I seemed obsessed with the need to view and photograph a leopard at close range, and it struck me one night that part of the obsession was due to my having heard the story of the man-eater of Punanai when I was twelve.

The more I thought about going back, the more I realized it would be an emotional journey. I couldn't go as a tourist, I couldn't go for a short trip, and I couldn't even go with others. It was as if I had to return alone in order to work something out in myself, to open myself to some experience, to discover what had kept me from visiting my homeland for forty years.

Of course I wanted to visit my sister Gillian, the only member of the immediate family still living in Sri Lanka. I wanted to see the tea estate where I had grown up and Rock Hill where I had known my grandfather best. I wanted to repeat the last trip I had made with my father, first south to Yala and then north to the ruined cities. Most of all, I wanted to go to Punanai to learn more about the man-eater. I wanted to peel off more of my corporate chains by moving freely in the open and in the jungle. I wanted to immerse myself in my own Old World, so that I could explore my roots and the meaning of my roots. I wanted to realize the past again, capture it, and bring it back to my family and my life in Canada. I also wanted to discover why suddenly I felt a need to come Home.

This need overrode all other considerations – even the threat of danger. Throughout the fall and winter of 1989, as I was getting ready to return, the newspapers were full of stories about Sri Lanka's civil war. Government troops were clashing with rebels, bombs were exploding in markets and buses, and innocent people were getting killed in the process. The country was a virtual powder keg. I knew I could get caught in the cross-fire between several warring factions, so I approached the journey with some trepidation.

Fear is a test that I have always tried to overcome in my life. Bob-sledding is quite dangerous, for example, and I was definitely keyed-up going into it as a member of the Canadian team that won a gold medal in the 1964 Winter Olympics, but I had to learn to push myself beyond nerves into a state where speed and winning are everything. I couldn't get into that state if I concentrated on the dangers more than on the goal. Even on the safari in Africa, when I was photographing lions up close or moving in on a leopard, I couldn't let fear set the agenda. So it was with Sri Lanka. If I wanted to go back, if I wanted to revisit Yala and get to Punanai, and if I wanted to understand the forces that were urging me to return, I had to cross the line between fear and achievement.

Why? Sir Richard Burton, the great Victorian explorer, once asked himself the same question. He was searching for the source of the Nile, "some thousand miles up a river, with an infinitesimal prospect of returning," when in his head the answer reverberated: "Damned fool. The devil drives!" I often used to remember that when I wondered what I was trying to accomplish. Certainly I wasn't looking for money or fame or comfort. Indeed, I was walking away from them by stepping beyond the boundaries I had worked so hard to create. Why place these strains on myself and my family?

Why put everything, including my life, at risk? Why hunt the sorrows of the past and expose them to the present? Why not continue leading a rich and sensible life? Maybe because it was adventurous, maybe because it was dangerous, maybe because it was a trial, maybe because it was unknown, maybe because it was ordained, or maybe because I was being driven by the devil.

There I was, sweating and afraid in the bathroom of the rest house at the edge of the jungle in the Sri Lankan night. I had been awakened by fear. There had been no footsteps, no gentle knock, but the handle of the door to my room had been turned. Someone was trying to get in. . . .

"Father, is that you?"

2
Colombo

On the way to the Toronto airport I got a speeding ticket, and even I had to ask: What's the rush? Two fortune-tellers had warned me that I would never see the Indian Ocean again – or, if I did, it would be with tragic consequences. I felt excitement, but also an uneasy sense of doom.

Amsterdam, Dhahran, Karachi, and down over the south of India, along the west coast of Sri Lanka, and into Colombo. Down from the brilliant sunrise above the clouds into an overcast and sticky morning. Down from the beautiful green patterns of rice paddies and coconut plantations into the crowded pandemonium of the Colombo airport.

The terminal was intensely hot and teeming with people either arriving in exhaustion or waiting with excitement. Amid the noise and confusion I noticed the silent men with the guns. Guns everywhere. And questions. Questions, questions, questions. About money. About my plans. About my sister. About my knife.

The customs officer had found the knife in my leather grip, which seemed quite regal amid all the cardboard boxes, sacks, plastic bags, tires tied together with string, and even some bird cages. The knife was evil-looking, and it was illegal. The official's pleasant face became very serious until I told him I had made both the knife and its primitive scabbard. Then he became curious, even friendly. He waved me through. Welcome home, Mr. Ondaatje.

A busy Colombo street scene.
Previous page: *Women working in the rice fields.*

Outside the airport, amid the turmoil of taxis and vans and bullock-carts and bicycles, as people pushed their way past soldiers and children and dogs and vendors in the warm rain, I found my sister Gillian and her daughter, Shaan. I had seen Gillian only once since I had left Ceylon as a boy, and it was good to join her at last in the place where we had been young and happy.

Those who have known the family have always claimed that Gillian and I are similar in looks and personality. She's outgoing and talkative, has a strong sense of history and family pride, and adores dramatic gestures. Her mathematical mind is directed towards contract bridge instead of finance, however, and she may be the worst driver Sri Lanka has ever seen. She can be brave and she can be difficult, and I soon saw both characteristics at work when she blasted and blustered her way through the military barricades on the road into Colombo. It was an absolute turmoil of cars criss-crossing, horns honking, motorbikes weaving, people shouting, and children begging. I couldn't believe Gillian didn't have an accident. As she drove, she was constantly accentuating

her thoughts with her right hand – outside the driver's window! – so that the drivers behind her never knew what she was intending to do; and at the height of her stories, the car often strayed dangerously across the highway's white centre line.

It took us more than an hour to journey the twenty-five miles from the airport at Katunayake to her house. The road was pot-holed and the traffic chaotic, teeming with pedestrians and cars, goats and carts, and I realized immediately how densely populated, congested, and hurried the city had become. Indeed, the population of the island had more than trebled since 1947 to almost eighteen million, which is a huge number for a country the size of Wales.

Perched on the shore by the Indian Ocean, Colombo now has a population of more than one million – mostly Sinhalese, but also Tamils, Muslims, Burghers (as the descendants of the European

My sister Gillian, whom I had seen only once since leaving Ceylon as a boy.

settlers are known), Chinese, and a smattering of foreign nationals. It has been a settlement since the eighth century, when Arab traders used it as a cinnamon port, but it was developed by the Portuguese, the Dutch, and the British. Though only a few Portuguese and Dutch buildings remain, the downtown area is still called the Fort from their days. In 1796 the British pushed out the Dutch, and most of Colombo was built in their colonial image. Now, I noticed,

People of every caste and creed, every trade and trick, all mingle and shout in the Pettah.

with a sense of dislocation, much of the colonial atmosphere had vanished.

Gillian's house is more Spanish than British in style, built around a large courtyard. It is on the outskirts of the city centre, but it feels as if it is in a village. It is engulfed day and night less by city noises than by village sounds: throat-clearing, chopping, bathing, shouts, conversations, the cackle of chickens and children, and the barking of dogs. Jet lag let me sleep for a couple of hours, but most nights I was awakened regularly by unfamiliar cries and movements.

Gillian is brave, but not foolhardy. Her husband, a naval officer and pilot, was working at the time in Saudi Arabia, and every night my sister took great care to protect the house. When I went to bed, I had to lock the door between the corridor and a small vestibule, then double-lock the door between the vestibule and my room. Gillian also locked herself behind two doors. Two servants slept on the floor in front of those doors in a living-room that was also locked. Outside, a gate was chained and locked too. When I asked Gillian why the servants slept on the living-room floor, she answered lightly, "Well, they have to sleep somewhere," but I knew perfectly well they were there to warn her of intruders. It made me feel a lot more vulnerable alone at the other end of the house.

I spent the afternoon driving around the city, visiting childhood haunts: the old Dutch fort, the Galle Face Hotel, the colonial government buildings, Horton Place where during the Second World War I had watched aerial dogfights between the Japanese and the British from the roof of my uncle's town house, and St. Thomas's Church where Ondaatjes had once preached. Later I went to the cemetery where my mother lies beside many Ondaatjes – but not my father, who is buried near my grandfather's estate in Kegalle. Some of the tombstones in the family plot go back to the seventeenth century. Gillian says she wants to be buried among the Ondaatjes, and I have left instructions for some of my ashes to be buried here too.

The Ondaatje name was very well known on the island, associated with public service and private achievement for almost three hundred years, and I had grown up proud of it and accustomed to its

Some of the gravestones of the Ondaatjes in the Colombo cemetery go back to the seventeenth century.

advantages. According to family lore, the first Ondaatje came to Ceylon in 1659 as a doctor summoned from India to cure the wife of the first Dutch governor, Adrian Van der Meyden. Most reports describe him as a physician to the king of Tanjore in southern India. Apparently, his cure succeeded where all others had failed. In gratitude the governor bestowed both appointments and land on Michael Jurgen Ondaatje, a name he apparently acquired then and there along with Christianity and a Portuguese wife. According to some, he had left behind another family in India or was to have a second family after the death of Magdalene de Croos, but their six children were the beginning of the Ondaatje dynasty.

Peter Philip Juriaan Quint Ondaatje, who became a lawyer and politician in Holland before being driven into exile.

Almost every Ondaatje of the second and third generation seems to have contributed something to the well-being of the island, particularly as professionals, intellectuals, and Christians. One was a translator in the Supreme Court under Dutch rule. One was rector of the Dutch Seminary; he was noted for translating the Old Testament into Tamil. The most famous was Peter Philip Juriaan Quint Ondaatje, who studied in Amsterdam, Utrecht, and Leyden, became a lawyer and politician in Holland, fought as a commanding officer against the Prussians before being driven into exile in France, waged a war of pen and sword on behalf of democracy and freedom for the Dutch people, and eventually returned to the East as a justice of the Supreme Court in Batavia. There were other Ondaatjes who discovered tin mines in Borneo, built fortifications in Java, and ran the famous botanical gardens in Ceylon. In the early nineteenth century Johan Jergen Ondaatje, an Anglican minister during the British regime, became the first colonial chaplain of St. Thomas's Church in Colombo. One of his sons became the first colonial Crown counsel, as well as a member of the Legislative Council, married the niece of the island's British attorney general, and fathered, among others, my paternal grandfather.

Philip Francis Ondaatje was a lawyer too, but his great success was as a businessman. When the British took over Ceylon from the Dutch, they began "opening up" the tea estates, a technical term that meant buying large tracts of land and making them available to the tea companies. What with the Portuguese and the Dutch and the inadequate village records, the titles to land up in the hills or out in the jungle weren't very clear. A lawyer with cunning and a grasp of the local language was obviously useful, and "Bampa" was such a lawyer. He worked for the various tea agencies, and sometimes he acted for his own account, accumulating badly titled property and selling it cleaned up. In

the process he became extremely wealthy. He retired on his fiftieth birthday and spent the rest of his days travelling the world, reading, and generally looking after his own affairs. I remember him well: stern, powerful, studious, often bad-tempered, very English in manner, and with a habit of grinding his teeth. He was always the boss, the head of the family, the one with the money, and I inherited my father's awe of him.

The darkness came early and suddenly, and by five there wasn't enough light to take any more photographs in the Pettah, the chaotic and congested bazaar near the Fort. It is not an area that you enter alone. It is a confusing maze of lanes filled with a pressing mass of people and is potentially dangerous. There are people of every caste and creed, every trade and trick, all mingling and shouting in a madhouse of commerce. One of the oldest parts of Colombo, the Pettah is also one of the poorest. It floods whenever it rains, and it reeks of rot in the heat. You have to haggle endlessly for everything, but if you are determined enough, you can get anything in the Pettah – clothes, trinkets, lorries, copper, tobacco, rope. You can even get killed.

Leaving the bazaar in a taxi, Shaan and I were stopped by three soldiers at an army checkpoint. They were armed with short-barrelled rifles, and one of them seemed to be looking for trouble. He was young, he barked orders in Sinhalese, and while he was searching my camera bag, he kept his finger on the trigger of his gun. He warned me, through Shaan, to keep my hands visible and not to make any rapid movements. Clearly I was suspect. Shaan and the driver were questioned severely and in detail about me. The jittery soldier began to relax only when I showed him – very slowly, very cautiously – my Canadian passport and tourist permit. It was dusk, the worst time to be out on the road.

I woke around four in the morning. It was still very dark, but there was a strange thudding outside my bedroom window – meal preparation in the kitchen of the next house. I had a cold shower and read till breakfast. I was reading an account of the famous Sathasivam murder case, which had been the talk of Colombo in the early 1950s. Uncle Noel, my mother's brother, had been the judge. A well-to-do woman was found brutally slain in the garage of her home, and the main suspect was her husband, Mahadevan Sathasivam, who

Soldiers in the Sri Lankan army. The army is a highly visible presence on the island.

37

had been one of Ceylon's greatest cricketers. He had the motive – he was in love with another woman, his wife was preparing to divorce him, he needed her money to continue his idyllic existence. However, he wasn't – and couldn't be proven – guilty.

"Go," my uncle had instructed the jury at the end of the trial, "and put this man out of his misery."

Uncle Noel and my mother had both been early risers, and I've heard that they spoke on the telephone for fifteen minutes every morning before breakfast. They adored each other. Like my grandmother, my mother had been very proud of Noel's success as a lawyer, then as a judge, then as attorney general of Ceylon. Though he remained a great figure in Ceylon's legal history, he retired to England on a pension that the government tried for a while to deny him.

My mother's brother, Noel Gratiaen, lawyer, judge, and eventually attorney general of Ceylon.

I spent the next morning battling bureaucrats, crowds, and the muggy heat. It took me two hours to get an extension of my thirty-day visa from two slow and unfriendly officials, and even cashing some travellers' cheques at a bank took lots of time and many more forms. I had a better sense of accomplishment after lunch, however, when I was shown a local collection of more than fifty antique knives. It took longer than four and a half hours to negotiate their purchase, but I got them all except for one Kandyan ceremonial dagger.

You need a knife in the jungle – to cut wood, to open coconuts, to peel fruit, to defend yourself – but my fascination with knives goes beyond their usefulness. Every different country has different people with different responsibilities, and every single person in the world has owned at least one knife at one time or another. All these countries and people and responsibilities have their own types of knives; moreover people use different kinds of knives at different times of their lives: penknives, dinner knives, carving knives, mat-weaving knives, hunting knives, ceremonial knives, army knives, knives plain or ornate. So knives are the culture and knives are the person.

I collect knives wherever I go. Once, driving across the southwestern United States, I found a black and broken Mexican knife in a little town north of Santa Fe. I fixed it and sharpened it and cleaned it, and engraved on its long

A Sinhalese fishwife bargaining in the market.

blade I discovered an epigram in Spanish: "Mientras al cielo no subas en la terra nos varemos." An almost literal English translation warns: "Until you are climbing into heaven, just remember you are still on earth." It is one of my favourite knives and is always on the desk in my study.

I was looking for knives in Sri Lanka too, because I knew it was an island of knives. Many villages have their own knife-maker. Each villager carries his own knife. The Sinhalese live by their knives, in the rice fields and jungles, and sometimes they die by their knives too. Knives are their chief instruments of attack and defence. When the man-eater of Punanai was finally killed, count-less stab wounds were found on its body, inflicted in futile panic by its victims.

My paternal grandfather, Philip Francis Ondaatje, a lawyer, had a great deal of commercial cunning.

I was almost too exhausted to eat, and all I want-ed to do was study my haul for hours, but dinner had been cooked by Alice, Gillian's family nanny, and it would have been impolite not to show my apprecia-tion of her gesture. In fact, she had travelled from the Kegalle area just to meet me. There are some important protocols in Sri Lanka involving loyal servants, and this was one of them. Though Alice had never known me, she was devoted to Gillian, and therefore she had come to Colombo to greet the brother from far away and cook me a meal, according to old tradition. In Canada I am sometimes known as Michael's brother, but here I was definitely known as Gillian's broth-er. Later I would have a similar honour of being received in Alice's own house and given another feast there. It was a remnant of the colonial system in which servants were treated as part of the family. The relationship goes beyond money and work. It evolves into genuine respect and complete responsibility. Unlike the current Western relationship between employer and employee, there is love and concern that reaches past the servants to their whole families when there is trouble or need. My own nanny went to look after my uncle Noel's family when most of us left Ceylon, and after my mother left my father, Nanny stayed on and nursed him through probably the worst period of his life, until he eventually remarried.

I basked that evening in the warmth of everyone's kindness and hospitality – a much more pleasant warmth than the humid heat that was causing me to drink tumblers of boiled and cooled water. All day, even when frustrated by

Sri Lanka is an island of knives. The Sinhalese live by their knives and sometimes die by their knives.

officialdom, I had been feeling delightfully "at home." The only nuisance was not being able to remember any Sinhalese, except for the odd word, for "matchbox" or "water." Not that I had ever been fluent. I had learned a little of the language at school and on the estate, but I lost it almost as soon as I was sent to England. In fact, I lost more than a language.

My father never trained me to become anything specific, but he always groomed me for an English education – what it would be like, how I must behave. Most important of all were good table manners. He used to be livid if he saw bad manners in his children. When I was twelve, he sent me to Blundell's, a British public school, to get, as he put it, "a decent education."

Leaving was traumatic for me in many ways, though I had already known exile from the estate when going to school first in Colombo and then in south India. The morning when I was to go, my mother fussed over me, which I loved and expected, but my father looked stern and very sad. I knew he had been crying. He pushed me up onto the step of the veranda, looked at me gruffly for a moment, then suddenly smothered me in a big hug. I could smell the stale drink on his breath and clothes, and I could feel him crying again. He didn't say anything. He just turned and went back into the house.

The boat trip from Ceylon to England took about three weeks, and I cried myself to sleep almost every night. When I got to London, the weather was cold and grey, the landscape was neither tropical nor familiar, and I was not thrilled.

I had been snatched from a pampered colonial society, a very privileged existence. I had a veneer of sophistication, but was still an unruly young boy. I had a thick black mass of hair, a sallow complexion, and a Bombay-Welsh accent that immediately made heads turn. I became very conscious of it and resolved at once to suppress it.

I arrived in the autumn term, the rugger term. Trials for the various junior teams started on my second afternoon. It was very cold, and probably felt even colder to me than it really was, but the other boys seemed happy to run around in thin sweaters. My hands were almost frozen and a deep chill shook my body. I was shoved into the scrum before I even knew what a scrum was. People began shouting orders at me, but I could only straggle behind, not knowing what to do. In that first practice I never even touched the ball, and most of the time I never even saw it. (I came to enjoy rugger reasonably well and participated in it enthusiastically enough, but it took me a long while to learn the game and longer to "think" the game.)

At the end of the practice we were covered with mud from head to toe, so it was off to the showers. Everybody stripped naked, piling boots, socks, rugger shorts, and jerseys into a heap outside the shower room, then lining up for turns under the water. There were about twenty of us, all naked and shivering on the cold cement floor. The water was no more than tepid. Afterwards we traipsed, with our skimpy towels around us, up to the "Big Dorm" where we got back into our jackets, flannels, and ties.

We were always being shunted around. There were always things to do and things to learn. We were "fags" – the most junior of junior boys in the school – and that meant that we were really servants to the most senior boys. They could order us to clean their shoes and boots, tidy their studies, make their beds, cook snacks for them, run errands for them, and generally be on "fag duty" every day except Sunday. I didn't mind that too much. I actually liked being told what to do while I was learning, and I had a very good "fag master." David Copplestone was a fair-haired, good-looking boy who was head of the house, captain of the house rugger team, and a first fifteen rugger colour. I was told flatly that I was very lucky to be his fag, and consequently I felt very proud. I flaunted this fact among the other new boys as a way of suggesting that I was someone special. I suppose I have tried to do the same kind of thing most of my life.

Thanks to cricket, I finally came into my own during the third term at Blundell's school in England.

At the end of the first ten days we were given a new-boys' test. I had had a "new bug" coach who was responsible for teaching me all sorts of useful and useless information. The height of the school tower (seventy-two feet). The date the school was founded (1604). The head of house. The captain of school rugger. The location of the river Lowman and Old Blundell's. What happened when the school foundation stone was flooded. (We were given a half-holiday.) The School Hags (the matrons). The Russell (the annual cross-country race). I passed with flying colours, which amazed my coach and myself, but I was still very much an outsider.

During the holidays I often went to stay with my father's sister Stephy, at Timberscombe. Aunt Stephy had married an Englishman, David Cockle, a vicar. He had rowed for Oxford and become a "Chindit" chaplain with General Orde Wingate's Phantom Army, the extraordinary British force that fought the Japanese behind their own lines in Burma. He was a very thoughtful and kind guardian. In the four difficult years after I left Ceylon he was my rock and mentor. Although I couldn't be as intimate with him as I had been with my mother and sometimes my father, I never hesitated to go to him when I needed advice or help – which was often.

At Timberscombe I worked on a local farm, shot rabbits for money, and bicycled to Dunster and Minehead to see my cousins Philip and Cecil, my aunt Enid's sons. It wasn't really lonely. Sometimes my sister Janet stayed; I had a home, regular meals, and a loving uncle and aunt. But it was never my place, and it was so very different from the wild, carefree life I had lived on the estate in Ceylon. Quite quickly I began to look forward to going back to Blundell's.

My second term was more successful. It was still cold, and I was still chilled to the bone, thin, and ungainly, with little apparent control of my limbs, but I had realized that to be fully accepted I had to be good at whatever I did. Not school work necessarily, but I had to be good at something. I finally came into my own in the third term, thanks to cricket.

I had learned it well at school in Ceylon, for cricket was, and still is, a mania there. Naturally, it became a mania with me too. I didn't have any cricket boots or white flannels for my first practice, but I did have a marvellous spell in the nets. When I knew the two junior-school cricket masters were watching, I kept my head down, got my left foot well out to the pitch of the ball, and drove everything along the ground without swiping or hooking. I knew this was my test, I knew I had to impress, and I did. I didn't say anything and I didn't fool around, and when the practice was over, I was told that I would be in the Junior Colt cricket squad. My stature rose almost immediately. I was somebody, I was useful.

House cricket matches were extremely important, and the house spirit was often far more intense than the school spirit. Boys began to pay attention to me, and I was invited to join make-up games of cricket or to go and watch matches. People asked my advice. What were Somerset's chances in the county championship season? What were England's chances? What was the Ceylon cricket team like? What was the Indian cricket team like? Had I ever seen the Australians play? Had I ever been to Lord's? Ceylon suddenly seemed far away. Life started to be fun. I was still a junior, still a fag, but there was a purpose to my being in England and being in school in England.

A few weeks later I was selected for the house first eleven. Put in to bat early, I scored eleven runs against bigger and more senior boys. I wasn't a bit afraid, even when their pace bowlers were on. It was a good beginning, and I was even congratulated by the captain.

Going on "away" matches for the Junior Colts was a particular pleasure. We skipped Saturday-morning lessons to go off by bus to Taunton, Sherbourne, Downside, or even Dartmouth to play other public schools. It was a thrill to be in our white flannels with boys from other schools, sitting down to a meal together, chatting, then playing against each other in matches that seemed terribly important. If you did particularly well, your achievements were proclaimed on the notice-board for the whole school to see. My name was posted a few times, and I glowed with pride.

As I grew more confident, I grew more secure. My school work improved, though I never reached great heights of scholastic achievement, and my cricket got better and better. I got house colours and school colours, and gradually the boys treated me more and more as one of them. Ceylon seemed farther and farther away, my parents more and more distant. I remembered them, of course, but their image was fading as my ambition increased. It was truly the making of an Englishman, and it was impossible not to become estranged from my native land.

At first I really missed going back. On holidays everyone else would be going home and I would be going somewhere else. That hurt, but I got used to it. I learned to be independent and to suppress my vulnerability. Blundell's became my home, in fact, and the 325 boys became a kind of family.

In 1947-48, shortly after my departure for England and Blundell's, Ceylon achieved its independence. So while I was being turned into an Englishman, Ceylon was undergoing a reverse process, being turned into Sri Lanka.

For eight years following Ceylon's independence, the island was governed by the United National Party (UNP), really an interracial coalition of moderate and Westernized elites dedicated to peace and stability. In the 1956 election, however, the UNP was replaced by the Sri Lanka Freedom Party (SLFP) under Solomon West Ridgeway Dias Bandaranaike. Although a member of the English-speaking elite, he had ties with the rural Sinhalese and knew how to harness Sinhalese nationalism under the slogan "Religion, Language, Nation." Nationalism had been growing as a political force for linguistic, cultural, religious, and economic reasons – fully supported by the anti-Western Buddhist resurgence of the 1950s, the wish to preserve the Sinhalese language and traditions, and the discontent of the village elites who resented the power of the new, urban elites. As unemployment rose, as agricultural land became scarcer, and as government jobs and contracts became harder to obtain, the Sinhalese majority turned against the United National Party – and its allies, the Ceylon Tamils.

The Tamils, though a minority concentrated in the north, had done well under British rule because of their hard work, intelligence, and fluency in English. Comprising only 18 per cent of the population, for example, they occupied more than 50 per cent of the civil service in 1956. Their numbers were also increasing thanks to the effective control of malaria; they were moving

into traditional Sinhalese territory. At the same time, the Sinhalese began coveting Tamil jobs. And naturally politicians exploited the resulting ethnic tensions for their own purposes.

The first act of the Bandaranaike government was to make Sinhalese the sole official language of Sri Lanka. The political effort to replace English with Sinhalese wasn't at all successful, in part because it cut Sri Lankans off from the mainstream of international trade and commerce, which still used English, in part because it provoked outrage among the Tamils, who saw it as an attack on their language, their culture, and their jobs, and an attempt to relegate them to second-class citizenship. The first response of the Tamils was passive resistance, but it led inexorably to ethnic violence that killed 150 people in 1956. Despite efforts at compromise, the island soon became polarized between Sinhalese nationalism in the south and Tamil nationalism in the north, as Tamil politicians demanded local autonomy and Sinhalese politicians continued to push the Sinhalese cause. Another round of violence broke out in 1958, and though order was restored under a state of emergency, tensions remained strong. There were arrests, assassinations, strikes, coups, and riots, including the killing of Bandaranaike himself by an extremist Buddhist monk in 1959.

Except for a five-year gap in the 1960s, Bandaranaike's party continued to rule, under the leadership of his widow and with the help of various coalitions, until 1977. It also continued to favour and promote Sinhalese culture and Buddhist tradition. Tamils had a tougher time getting into university or into the civil service, and by 1980 their share of the bureaucracy had dropped to 11 per cent.

Sri Lankan history has always been dominated by intermittent wars between the Sinhalese and the Tamils. Both groups originally came from India hundreds of years before Christ. The Sinhalese, fair-skinned Buddhist Indo-Aryans from the north, arrived first, but were followed two hundred years later by the Tamils, dark-skinned Dravidian Hindus from the south. Each has oppressed the other at different periods under various kings. (Their symbols are the lion and the tiger, though neither cat exists on the island.) It wasn't until the 1970s, however, that a modern Tamil military force emerged. In 1972, seventeen-year-old Velupillai Prabakaran organized twenty-nine other Tamil teenagers into a guerrilla movement called the Liberation Tigers of Tamil Eelam (LTTE), or the Tamil Tigers. Their goal was to establish an independent Tamil nation in northern Sri Lanka. They were products of the Tamil Youth Movement, which in turn had been nurtured by the Tamil United Liberation Front (TULF). Eventually, the TULF leaders were murdered, thus

Buddhism, by far the most prevalent religion in Sri Lanka, is practised by more than two-thirds of the population.

destroying the organization that had spawned the LTTE.

Meanwhile, in 1977 the Sinhalese nationalist Freedom Party was ousted by a revived United National Party under the seventy-one-year-old J.R. Jayewardene, a passionate believer in a free market economy and in Western progress, a tolerant Buddhist who had been born a Christian, and an idealistic optimist about Tamil nationalism. Unfortunately, neither his government nor the Tamil parliamentary opposition could gather the support of the extremists on both sides, and no peaceful resolution seemed possible. In 1983, just at the point when Sri Lanka struck most investors and tourists as a sane, safe, and well-educated tropical paradise, civil war erupted. Prabakaran, now twenty-eight, and a band of other Tamil Tigers ambushed a Sri Lankan army convoy near Jaffna and killed thirteen soldiers. In other outbreaks, more Sinhalese were killed in the north and east. That set off an explosion of Sinhalese rage in which security forces and youth gangs killed more than a thousand Tamils, destroyed Tamil homes and businesses, and terrorized innocent Tamils all over the island.

The immediate effect, of course, was to increase popular support for the Tigers among ordinary Tamils. Their numbers went from about five hundred into the thousands; they became better armed and better trained; their activities expanded into robberies, executions, assassinations, raids, and disruption of democratic elections; and the idea of a Tamil nation, previously just a dream, became a necessary goal. Prabakaran himself became a legend: unconfirmed stories were told of how, at the age of four, he had seen his uncle being

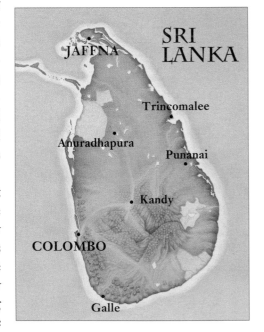

burned alive; how, despite coming from the fisherman caste and dropping out of school, he had become a sophisticated political leader well-versed in the ancient epics of the Hindu kings and warriors; how, despite his admiration for Napoleon and Castro, he remains an austere and sober Tamil nationalist. His followers call him Thamby, "little brother."

By August 1983, the government effectively had lost control of the north to the Tigers. By 1987, the only prospect seemed endless fighting, as negotiations failed repeatedly and the death toll mounted daily, finally reaching 10,000. More unsettling still, the Tigers had a powerful base across the water in India, just two hundred miles away in the state of Tamil Nadu, and they seemed to have found a strong ally in New Delhi. For Indira Gandhi, supporting the Tigers made her government popular with India's own Tamils, and turmoil in Sri Lanka could only increase India's influence in the region. Certainly the Tigers were allowed to find refuge in India and to be trained, financed, equipped, and advised there.

In 1985, after Rajiv Gandhi succeeded his mother as prime minister, India's Sri Lankan policy became more ambivalent. Rajiv Gandhi didn't move against the Tamil Tigers in India, but he did proclaim his opposition to an independent Tamil state on the island. He even tried to force a compromise agreement between the Tigers and Jayewardene that would grant new powers and protections to Sri Lanka's Tamils. The initiative failed to get the support of Prabakaran, however. In April 1987, two terrorist attacks against innocent Sinhalese – one killing 128 people pulled from three buses, the other killing 113 people in Colombo's Pettah market – were interpreted as the Tigers' response. The possibility of a compromise faded. A month later Jayewardene ordered a full military offensive in the north.

Through the army, the government eventually was able to gain temporary control over part of the north, but at a terrible political, economic, and human cost. India intervened, sending food and supplies to the Tamils; whole villages were destroyed, resulting in thousands of civilian deaths and thousands of refugees; and an estimated $1.3 million was spent each day to conquer the northern part of the country. Jayewardene found himself under attack by his international allies, from the business elite already suffering because of the low world price of tea, and from the more extreme Sinhalese nationalists. Chief among the latter were the Janatha Vimukthi Peramuna (JVP), an outlawed movement of anti-Tamil terrorists preaching an odd mixture of Trotskyism, nihilism, and nationalism. By 1987 the JVP had weapons, about two thousand members, and quiet sympathy among many powerful and ordinary Sinhalese.

Despite pressure from New Delhi and Washington for negotiations, peace proved elusive. The moderate Tamils had been expelled from parliament for refusing to swear their opposition to a separate Tamil state. The government security forces attacked the Tamil militants, pushing them further towards extremism. And the Tamil Tigers reacted with their own terrorist campaigns, in the absence of any other effective voices among the Tamils. By June 1987, however, worried about separatist movements in its own country, India pressed for a resolution, to the extent of putting some distance between itself and Prabakaran's hard-line violence. A month later New Delhi and Colombo reached an agreement, providing for a new, semi-autonomous Tamil province and a military de-escalation by all sides under the supervision of the Indian Peace-Keeping Force (IPKF). Again, however, Prabakaran refused to consent.

A civil war, the Sri Lankan army in the south, the Tamil Tiger rebels in the north, the Indian army in between for good or evil – so far a nasty and prolonged conflict, but not particularly complicated. By December 1988, however, there were new factors: rival Tamil factions such as the Tamil National Army in the north, rival Sinhalese factions such as the anarchist JVP in the south, and the desire of both the Tamil Tigers and the Sri Lankan government to get rid of the 60,000 Indian troops. The Indian Peace-Keeping Force had gone to war against the Tigers for control of the north as part of its agreement with Colombo and was even reported to be backing the Tigers' rivals with training and arms; at the same time, its brutal behaviour and self-serving interference in the island's affairs also alienated the Sinhalese. Late in 1988 Jayewardene was succeeded as president by his prime minister, Ranasinghe Premadasa. A hard-working, self-made astute politician, Premadasa was determined to rid the island of its strife by improving the economic conditions of the rural poor. He was able to get the IPKF removed by March 1990.

Just the anticipation of the pull-out increased the tensions and the complexity of the situation. The government had to have thorough control of the southern areas in order to be able to move its troops into the vacuum created in the north; the Tigers had to increase their struggle for supremacy over their Tamil challengers; the two groups faced each other in a military contest once more. This was the violent confusion into which I had walked: Tamils fighting Tamils, Sinhalese fighting Sinhalese, and almost everyone trying to oust the Indians.

Despite a general news blackout, snippets of horrible information about killings and conflicts reached us constantly, through small items in the newspapers or bits of hearsay. There were warnings at every turn about the dangers of doing this or that, or going here or there, as I travelled around searching for leopards or retracing my journey with my father. My safari to the man-eating leopard of Punanai became a safari to the Tamil Tigers, and my quest to understand my father's troubled life and to fit together the jumbled pieces of my past was shadowed by the turbulence of an ongoing political upheaval.

After my parents were divorced, my mother left Sri Lanka for England. She felt, however, that my sister Gillian would have far better educational opportunities in Sri Lanka than we could have afforded for her in England, so Gillian stayed on, living in the home of family friends, Hamish and Jill Sproule.

During my visit, the Sproules' son Michael came by one evening for drinks and dinner. He was more like a brother to Gillian than a friend. Michael was a well-known lawyer; and like his mother's brothers, he was an excellent sportsman.

Derek de Saram, his uncle, had played cricket at Oxford and captained the Ceylon team, while Koo de Saram had been a great tennis player for the island. The great achievement of my brother Michael's superb book *Running in the Family* was to re-create the world of the Ondaatjes, Sproules, and de Sarams, even though he had been too young to remember it in its heyday. Through interviews and research, by travelling back to Ceylon in reality and in his imagination, he painstakingly assembled the pieces of the puzzle that had been the Somerset Maugham existence of Colombo high society at the cusp, just before it collapsed into nothingness. And he got it right: the mood, the irresponsibility, the jazz, the frivolity, and the ultimate uselessness. Even when he exaggerated certain facts, he remained truthful to their spirit.

Over prawn curry Michael Sproule and I talked mostly about the negative effects of the civil war on the economy. War always breeds inflation, and that was particularly true in Sri Lanka's case because the foreign aid on which it relies had been reduced, mostly on the questionable grounds that the government was depriving the minorities of their rights. Inflation was running above 20 per cent a year then, and the price of rice rose 30 per cent during my stay. And because people were moving away from paper money, real estate was expensive. Though remote properties were still cheap, houses in Colombo and coconut estates near the city were worth North American prices, which is staggering in a Third World economy. There was still a tea industry and a textile industry, but foreign aid and money from overseas relatives made greater contributions to the gross national product, and the tourism industry had been destroyed just as it was on the verge of rivalling that of Thailand and Hong Kong. From the outside it appeared that Sri Lanka was engaged in a deliberate act of self-destruction.

After dinner and well into the night I caught up on Gillian's family news. She told me, for example, of a distant cousin who had drunk himself to death. A young and clever lawyer, he had fallen into despair after his father became involved in some financial scandal and was jailed. The shame probably destroyed him. I could feel more sympathy for him than anybody could possibly know.

My father was the only son, the youngest of three children, quite a bit younger, in fact, than Aunt Enid and Aunt Stephy. He was a big man, with sandy hair and blue eyes, bigger than his own father, and he was incredibly charismatic. He could lead anybody anywhere; he could sell anybody anything. He was a major in the Ceylon Light Infantry, he was fluent in Sinhalese and Tamil, and he was a very good planter. For a long time he worked hard and well, managing estates for Carson, Cumberbatch and Co. Ltd., helping with my grandfather's estates, and leading the planters' association in the Ratnapura district. I remember him traipsing mile after mile, day after day, up and down the slopes.

In his youth, it's true, he had a wild period, characterized by extravagant fun and drunken escapades. Much of it can be put down to his age and to the age in which he was young – both were carefree and indulged – though some of it might have been a reaction against his father's intimidation. Unfortunately, he never got over the habit of drink. For most of the time that I knew him he was completely sober, but occasionally he went on a binge. He would start drinking as soon as he got up, then fall asleep from ten o'clock until three in the afternoon, do a little work until about six, then go back to sleep for the night. When he was drunk, no one could predict

Philip Mervyn Ondaatje. My father was a big man who could lead anybody anywhere and sell anybody anything.

what he would do, and we all feared him, just as he was feared on the estate. These bouts got worse and more frequent after I left for Blundell's.

In many ways my brother Michael's book is a love letter to the father he never knew, a large and glamorous man away in the distance. But I had been deeply involved with that man, and I had had to grapple with his demons, which never seemed either romantic or amusing. I had helped to carry him to bed at ten in the morning. I had had to watch him walk naked along the river where he might easily have drowned. I had been in the car with him and my two sisters when he had driven to the edge of a steep precipice. I had had to make the decision to leave the car, with my sisters in it, to get help. In Michael's book this incident became rather light-hearted, as my sisters argued over who was the heavier and who could get out to fetch help without sending the car plunging off the road. At the time there was only terror. I was in the front seat. My father had passed out. The front right wheel below him was dangling in mid-air.

In 1948 Ceylon became independent, along with India and Pakistan. The entire investment climate changed in the face of increased government taxation, while the ready market of British companies selling their own tea into Britain became much more difficult. My family collapsed at the same time. My father sank deeper into debt and drink, my mother left him and was forced to work in Colombo, and I learned far away in England about their divorce and our downfall.

Just before my last year, I received my mother's letter. She told me that I couldn't continue at Blundell's because we simply didn't have any more money! I had had no idea of the family's financial troubles. Like most privileged children, I didn't think about things like that. Things had finally been going so well at school, and now I had to leave before experiencing the best years of school life, as a senior. In some ways the shock of being forced out of my second home was more brutal than that of being sent away from Ceylon.

By coincidence I had tea the next day with Michael Sproule's former wife, Khemi, and her husband, Ajita da Costa, a successful businessman and active supporter of many cultural organizations in Sri Lanka. She is a beautiful and talented dancer who specializes in the traditional dances of Kandy. Mother, too, used to perform this intricate and exquisite art, before she was introduced to the free form of Isadora Duncan. My mother actually earned her living as a dancer in Colombo before my father swept her away to the foothills. The Sproules, Gillian, my mother: they all seemed to be bound by their own dance in my mind.

When my mother left to join my sister Janet and me in England, there had been strong reasons for having Gillian remain in Colombo with the Sproules. She was doing exceptionally well at school, there was no way we could have afforded a decent education for her in England, and she seemed so happily settled that my mother didn't want to uproot her.

Now, however, Gillian shared with me the hurt and anger she had experienced at the time. She had felt left behind, without money or pride. She had lost her family, and she had never understood why.

Night noises. All night. What with the dogs and cats, the birds, and the mosquitoes, I barely slept. Even in a nation of early to bed and early to rise, I always seemed to be the first one up. And I couldn't wait to get going. There was so much to do. The days were a hot haze of shopping for supplies and equipment to take on the expedition. In the evenings we progressed from cocktails to curries, to long conversations about politics and business. Then another humid and restless night behind the locked doors. Night noises. I longed for the jungle.

One evening, as a diversion, I went to the British Council to hear Richard Murphy, the Irish poet, read from his newest collection. Murphy had been born in Ceylon, and his book *The Mirror Wall* contained poems based on the famous graffiti scrawled on the shiny surface of rock in the high fortress at Sigiriya. The poems weren't bad, but the translations of the graffiti I had read in the classic two-volume edition by Dr. Senarath Parnavitana were much better. The original versions had a simplicity, a melody, and a brilliant humour that in my opinion Murphy couldn't match. I was also, to my surprise, annoyed that this *outsider* was fiddling around with *my* island's heritage. Nor did I miss the delicious irony that the high commissioner was David Gladstone, a descendant of the British prime minister who had provoked so much trouble on Murphy's own island. Would Sri Lanka's troubles go on as long as Ireland's?

I had recently met Nihal Fernando, Sri Lanka's best-known photographer, and we became instant friends, not least because we shared a passion for nature portraits. Slightly older than I, he is a sensitive and popular individual, and he helped me with contacts and advice. He had endless tales about Yala, finding leopards, being chased by an elephant, fishing, birds, photography, game wardens, government officials, the wilderness. He was a man of the wilderness, and he clearly loved Sri Lanka more than any other place on earth.

I was visiting Nihal for a tour of his photography and publishing business when he told me he had heard that an Ondaatje had killed himself in Canada. Two thoughts raced through my head. One possibility was that the rumour was about me – that reports of my death were being spread by someone as a warning to me not to write about or meddle in Sri Lankan politics. If I should disappear or be found dead, the news would fit the rumour. Given the powder-keg nature of Sri Lankan politics, it wasn't such a crazy idea. But the second possibility was that something had happened to my brother, Michael.

Fear about Michael put me into a frenzy. When I pressed Nihal for more information, he could tell me only, "I heard it from a guest at a party at the high commissioner's."

Totally panicked, unable to think of anything else, I frantically began sending telexes to Canada to try to trace Michael. Hours passed with no response. I was to have dinner that evening with Nihal, Richard Murphy, and a former head of the wildlife department. I tried to put on a show of normalcy, but it was no use. I was totally distracted.

Late in the evening, I got a call from my Bermuda office. "Find Michael!" I shouted into the poor connection, which soon broke off altogether.

Another two hours of torment went by. Then the phone rang. "Christopher?"

said a faint voice from the other side of the world. "It's Michael." A wave of relief flooded through me. I can compare it only to the tremendous feeling of release on waking from a terrifying dream.

It was an intensely emotional call. I spoke to him, Gillian spoke to him, even Nihal spoke to him, though they had never met. We all wanted to hear Michael's voice. To make sure.

Later on, when I got back to Canada, I realized that Michael's name had been confused in the transmission, mistaken for that of the well-known Canadian critic Ken Adachi, who had indeed tragically killed himself.

Nihal Fernando introduced me to Lyn de Alwis, who had formerly been the head of Sri Lanka's wildlife department. I had known Lyn at school, at St. Thomas's College in Colombo, although he was senior to me. He had been a champion shot-putter and had grown into a strong and conscientious man with a great knowledge of wildlife. He had lost his job through some political

Nihal Fernando, Sri Lanka's best-known photographer and the author of many books about wildlife.

changes, but he was still widely consulted in Sri Lanka and abroad. He gave me some free advice:

Beware of mosquitoes. They carry a dangerous strain of malaria. Use citronella oil to repel them. Never wear black shirts, which attract them.

Beware of long grass, because of snakes. Never wear sandals.

Beware of certain parts of Yala, because of terrorists. Stay on the main tracks.

Warnings about malaria and snakes, I expected. But terrorists? Lyn reported that the fighting had moved recently to the edges of the park. There was now a real danger of getting caught in the cross-fire.

Last-minute shopping for provisions. At Yala we would get a bungalow, but we had to bring in food, kerosene, and safari equipment. There would be some chicken, fish, fruit, and coconuts available locally – a good thing, since the refrigerator turned out to be useless, except as a safe box against ants and animals – but we packed the jeep with everything else: rice, cereal, powdered milk, tea, spices. Also our clothes, camera bags, and camping gear.

The night before our departure my adrenalin was pumping so much that I couldn't get to sleep at all. I was just too excited. Finally I took a sleeping pill.

Meat vendors on the highway.

3
Yala

I was like a child on Christmas morning, dressed and ready to go before breakfast. Adding to the feeling of childlike enthusiasm was the association with my twelve-year-old self heading off on this same trip with my father. I went with these ghosts back to the jungle.

I also went with Lakshman Senatilleke, a lawyer in his forties and one of Gillian's bridge competitors. He had heard about my expedition and offered to drop everything to drive me around Sri Lanka in his Willys jeep. He had that sort of pleasant enthusiasm. It had taken him up and down in life, apparently, and after gambling away his family's property he had settled down to practising law – in the intervals between adventures. I called him Lucky.

My other travelling companion was Childers Jayawardhana, a former warden at Yala. He was older, quieter, and more reserved than Lucky, but still remarkably youthful for a man in his sixties. Lucky certainly loved the wild; but Childers had the cool, calm manner of a true naturalist. He was not only an expert on the birds of Yala, he was also in the middle of writing a book about the park, so I was fortunate to have him as a guide. He knew everyone who could be useful, he knew every corner that would be exciting, and he knew something about leopards.

Running in the Family is well known in Sri Lanka, and it tends to confirm the Ondaatjes' reputation as an amazing, extroverted, and somewhat bohemian family of achievers. When an Ondaatje gets involved in something, people aren't sure if he will be brilliant or mad. According to Gillian, she had asked one particular acquaintance to guide me on my trip, and he was all set to go

A young Sri Lankan soldier on manoeuvres.
Previous page: *Sambur at dawn.*

· ANNO · MDCLXIX ·

until he read Michael's book. "Christ!" he had exclaimed. "The Ondaatjes are notorious, and this guy from Canada is going to be the same!" So he refused to come.

Lucky and Childers arrived by six. We loaded our luggage and sixteen boxes of supplies into the jeep, had a meal that seemed too long to me, and left Gillian sipping her morning tea. We stopped to pick up our hired driver, Mahinda Rajapakse (known as Raja), and drove out of the city as if on some extraordinary picnic. The streets were already busy, so our start seemed painfully slow, but eventually Colombo dissolved into a string of villages stretching south along the western coast: Panadura, Kalutara, Bentota, Ambalangoda, Hikkaduwa, Dodanduwa.

It was a straight road lined with coconut trees and often skirting the ocean. Mostly it ran among fields and huts until it cut through the centres of village life. We stopped only to take photographs – of a local cricket match, of fishermen, of faces – or to look for old knives. Generally we used the time to get to know each other, discussing such things as our schooling, our cameras, Canada. By noon we were in Galle, a beautiful old-world town on the island's southwest corner.

Cricket was, and still is, a passion in Sri Lanka.
Opposite page: The Dutch East India Company coat-of-arms above an archway near the ramparts in Galle.

Much of Galle is actually contained within the fort that had been built by the Portuguese in 1589 and enlarged by the Dutch in 1640. For centuries Galle had been an important port for the spice trade between the Middle East and the Orient, though now it is better known for its well-preserved ramparts, its spacious Dutch houses, its romantic history, and the colonial comfort of the New Oriental Hotel, which is more like a large house, full of antiques and quaint atmosphere. As children we used to visit Galle regularly, particularly when Uncle Noel occupied one of the judges' bungalows there, and I associated it with many happy memories. For all that I was anxious to press on to Yala.

Driving along the south coast we came by good fortune upon an annual village canoe race. There were dozens of people and huge excitement at the water's edge as two dugouts competed against each other. But that was our only stop until we got to Weligama, where my family had come often for holidays. I almost wept as images from those times returned with remarkable vividness. The town was busier, the highway was wider, but the place still had its peace and its charm – though I was disappointed not to find any prawns available at the rest house. I had been remembering them as a childhood delicacy all morning.

Offshore a little way was the island of the Count de Mauny, a Frenchman whose house my family had rented for a couple of Easters. It was an attractive building on a rise of the island, with big windows on three sides looking out to the ocean. My father especially had loved its isolation and tranquillity.

Along the road we could still see examples of Dutch or British architecture in some of the great colonial houses. Most of them had been taken over by government officials, but there remained some old families, sitting among old maps and old books and old objects, often without a proper water system, but desperately clinging to the glories of the past. Many of them have a crest or a coat of arms over their doors as a reminder of the days when the colonial authorities entrusted them with some local responsibilities.

We met a local burgher, a descendant of the Dutch who had stayed and intermarried. He was an expert on old families, and when I asked him if there were any Ondaatjes around, he said, "You mean the Ondaatjes from Kegalle? I think they've all gone to Canada." I then introduced myself and we talked about my grandfather, whom he had known when he was a child.

There wasn't much time for chatting, however. Dusk was coming, and at dusk it was advisable to be off the roads.

My mother was a Gratiaen, and the Gratiaens were a very proper Dutch burgher family. In truth, however, she believed herself to be English, and was one of those anglophiles who manage to be more English than the English. Her children had to dress in English clothes – which we hated – and speak with an English accent. Even the domestic help in the bungalow were not allowed to speak anything other than English in our presence.

My mother, Doris (née Gratiaen) Ondaatje, and my father. Their charmed existence had a fantastic, make-believe quality.

It wasn't a matter of pretending to be English. It was a compulsion to be English in our manners, our clothes, and our thoughtfulness. Thus, we were allowed to go to the Hill Club in Nuwara Eliya if we were properly turned out, but we weren't allowed to talk once we got there.

Along with her gifts as a dancer, my mother had a highly developed sense of drama – of theatre. Her children became her players, and the drawing-rooms and clubs of colonial Ceylon became her stage. In my memory she was always outgoing, loving, and attentive. Always around, always generous, always reliable, always doing "the right thing," and always living beyond her means. As a dancer with Uncle Noel's first wife, Dorothy Clementi-Smith, she had been the belle of many parties and the subject of many zany tales. When my father plucked her from the busy Colombo scene and took her to the wilderness up country, she must have missed the energy and fun, because she always seemed to be talking about those lost days.

She was like an exotic bird of paradise spotted in an often gloomy jungle, and though my father seemed only to tolerate her madness and showmanship, I sensed he was secretly proud of the fun and chaos she created around him. In this way, they were made for each other, and we who were the products of their union became part of their conspiracy against the rest of the world – and sometimes against each other.

It wasn't hard to guess where much of my mother's spirit had come from: her own mother, the irrepressible and outrageous Lalla. Large, fair-skinned, with angular features and billowing dresses, my grandmother was one of the well-known wonders of the time. Constantly showing up when least expected, hopping from one home to another and one project to another, with no money and a head full of wacky ideas, she made everyone laugh – though my father usually hid his laughter behind a façade of disapproval.

Sometimes Lalla's eccentricities were really embarrassing. Once I was walking with her around the tea estate when I noticed that she had fallen behind.

Dashing back to see what was the matter, I found her urinating in the middle of the road – standing up, with her feet apart and her skirt pulled up above her knees. When I recalled this at dinner one night at the de Sarams', a cousin added that, worse still, Lalla had done the same thing in the middle of the playground at Bishop's College in Colombo.

In my brother's book, Lalla dies when she is carried off in the great Nuwara Eliya flood. It is a marvellous piece of literature and true to her zany character, but in fact she died of alcohol poisoning. She and her brother had been out drinking, and Lalla simply never woke up. That is a sadder and more depressing account than Michael's. Nor was there much charm in seeing that crazy and eccentric old woman sitting on a stool in the busy, chaotic Nuwara Eliya market bragging to bemused strangers about her son, my uncle, then the attorney general of the island.

My maternal grandmother, Lalla, was an inveterate gambler and a noted eccentric.

From Galle, we continued on to Hambantota, at the beginning of the flat, dry, yellowy-brown scrubland that I love so much. It is another place where my family went to holiday on the beach, and to use as a base for excursions into Yala or the Wirawila Bird Sanctuary. I have kept a special place in my heart for Hambantota – as did Leonard Woolf, who was a colonial agent there from 1908 to 1911. (He was not quite thirty years old, but weighed down by ninety volumes of Voltaire.)

My father never drank there, or at least I have no recollection of his being drunk at Hambantota. Instead, I saw him as quiet and content, watching his children running on the beach among the fishermen and their boats. There was a pier, but I found boys fishing off the stumps of the old one from which I too had fished, and I heard once again the unique smacking sound that the sea made as its waves rose and fell on the beautiful curved beach. How often had I gone to sleep to that sound! I had never forgotten it, in England or in Canada, and I was astonished to read in Leonard Woolf's *Sowing* that it had made the same impression on him.

A boy fishing off the broken pier foundation at Hambantota.

All year round day and night, if you looked down that long two-mile line of sea and sand, you would see, unless it was very rough, continually at regular intervals a wave, not very high but unbroken two miles long, lift itself up very slowly, wearily, poise itself for a moment in sudden complete silence, and then fall with a great thud upon the sand. That moment of complete silence followed by the great thud, the thunder of the wave upon the shore, became part of the rhythm of my life.

One day at Hambantota, when I was ten or eleven, I was passing the time on a rainy morning whittling a piece of wood with my knife. I cut through both the wood and the thumb of my left hand. The top part of the thumb was hanging by a piece of skin. I could see the back of my nail. Blood gushed out. I put the top of the thumb back in place, went into my room, and found a blue balloon, which I tugged over the thumb to keep it together. Then I went to my father.

"I've cut my thumb," I said as matter-of-factly as possible. "What should I do?"

"Put it under running water," he said, not realizing how serious it was. So I put the blue thing under a stream of rain-water that was falling from the roof. The gutter ran with red blood and blue dye. There was no improvement, of course, so I went back to my father and told him to take me to a doctor.

The doctor looked at the balloon and said I would get blood poisoning from the dye, but when he peeled it off, the top of my thumb seemed to have stuck onto the rest of it. "We might as well take a chance," the doctor said. He stitched what he could and hoped for the best.

The graft held, I didn't die from blood poisoning, and almost fifty years later I showed Lucky and Childers the gruesome scar.

Before leaving Hambantota after tea, we were warned to hurry along and get to the Tissamaharama rest house before dark. The "Tissa" rest house was situated in an especially peaceful spot, on the edge of the Wirawila Bird Sanctuary. It was hard to realize that only a few weeks before several hundred JVP rebels had been killed in the area. Bodies were still being found along the coast road.

Lakshman Senatilleke, lawyer, wildlife enthusiast, and raconteur – and a wonderful travelling companion.

The Tissamaharama rest house was a long bungalow owned by the Ceylon Hotels Corporation and kept for the use of travelling officials and paying guests. It had rooms opening out to a veranda and a central dining-room between the two wings.

After we checked in, a servant carried our bags down a long corridor and up a flight of winding, stone steps. Then we traversed another long corridor to the very end of the building. Childers and Lucky immediately announced that they would share a room, so I was left by myself, farthest from everyone else. That didn't make me very comfortable. From my window I saw five armed soldiers in the grounds below. Apparently there was a government minister staying overnight. Instead of making me feel safer, his presence made me more worried, for if he were a target of attack, we could be accidental victims.

For a while I contemplated the sunset view of the tank, one of the ancient man-made reservoirs that dot Sri Lanka like small lakes. This tank, restored from a ruinous state by the British in the late nineteenth century, had been built by King Maha Naga two centuries before Christ. Barely a hundred years later, however, it had begun to fall into disrepair and be swallowed by the jungle. For the Kingdom of Ruhuna went into decline soon after its greatest king,

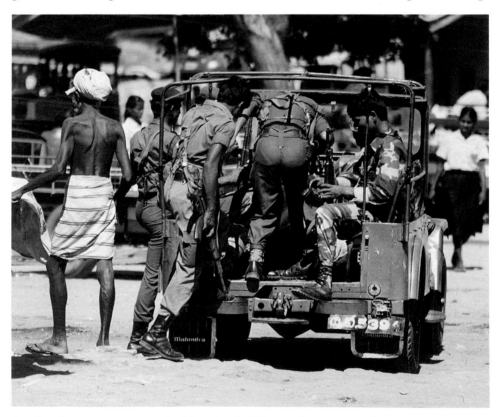

Sri Lankan army jeeps and soldiers in the Tissamaharama market.

70

Duttha Gamini, led his army north to Anuradhapura, to drive out the Cholas, a Hindu tribe from southern India. Such was Duttha Gamini's fervour as a young man to defeat the Cholas that he had accused his own father of cowardice and been exiled from Ruhuna until after the old king's death. In modern times his fervour had served as the inspiration for the drive to expel the Indian Peace-Keeping Force from Sri Lanka's shores.

I went down to dinner, lingered a bit for a chat with Childers and Lucky, and then the three of us went to our rooms through the dimly lit halls. I locked my door, washed, and crawled under the moth-eaten mosquito netting, which quickly proved itself useless. I was bitten mercilessly by mosquitoes. It was a hot night, absolutely dark, and there were constant noises: voices murmuring outside the window, steps on the gravel drive, the alarmed shriek of birds, dogs barking, jeeps arriving and leaving, occasional staccato commands in Sinhalese. I couldn't sleep at all.

Around two in the morning I heard the handle of the door to my room turn. It might have been a security guard, but I didn't think so. I had heard no footsteps. The handle turned again, and this time the door itself was pushed. Stealthily I crept out of bed and into the bathroom, locking its door. I must have stayed there, leaning against the cold stone wall, attentive to the slightest noise, for twenty minutes. When nothing more happened, I ventured back to bed, only to be attacked again by the curiously silent mosquitoes.

I didn't sleep more than a couple of hours, but was up at five feeling neither tired nor afraid. I waited impatiently for the sun to come up over the Tissa tank. When it did, with a silent and breath-taking beauty, I saw a young boy in a sarong raking leaves from the lawn. He was where the five soldiers had been. I rushed down to the veranda to admire the morning light with him. I couldn't imagine what he thought I was doing, but I felt secure to be near his simple raking. Herons and other water birds flew over the large tank across the pink and yellow horizon.

When Childers and Lucky showed up for breakfast an hour later and asked me how I had slept, I lied. I was supposed to be a fearless adventurer, after all, and my terrors seemed silly in the daylight. As we went to have our egg rulang and string hoppers I saw the boy still raking. I had the oddest sensation that my life was just starting again.

By eight o'clock it was hot, the sun almost unbearable. We drove into the village to get chicken and fish before heading into the Yala park. In the market were several army jeeps full of soldiers who seemed very uneasy. They were eyeing us closely. We stood out, of course, even though we tried to be discreet.

The road between Tissa and Yala was reported to be frequented by JVP terrorists. So when we found it blocked by a tree, we became suspicious of an ambush. The tree certainly looked as if it had been blown up rather than blown over. Later we heard that two JVP members from a nearby village had been killed and their bodies placed inside tires in the middle of the road and set on fire. Whenever we came to army checkpoints, there were always piles of tires prominently displayed beside them. Was this some kind of silent warning?

With the road blocked, we had to make a circuitous, six-mile detour along the narrow paths between water tanks and rice paddies. The landscape was beautiful, but whenever we stopped to ask directions, we found the people strangely hostile. We were alone in uncharted territory, oversensitive to signs of ambush, and we were relieved to get back on to the main road.

Almost as soon as we entered Yala's arid and sandy terrain, we saw spotted deer, wild buffalo, peacocks, and elephants. Yala is really a group of five parks, covering almost four hundred square miles. It emerged from the reserve set up at the turn of the century by British sportsmen interested in controlled hunting. Its first warden was Henry Engelbrecht, an acquaintance of Leonard Woolf.

Old H.H. Engelbrecht had come to Ceylon from South Africa as a prisoner of war in 1905. Because he wouldn't swear allegiance to the British Crown (on the grounds that he knew only the present king, not the successors), he wasn't allowed to return home, so he stayed on. He apparently had three local wives and numerous children, but he wasn't much liked. In fact, Woolf described him as "hated," as well as "obstinate," "very stupid," and "completely without fear and without nerves." Tough and cruel, he was known to whip villagers, and he controlled his subordinates with an iron hand. In revenge the locals beheaded his prize bulls and murdered his pet bear cub. During the First World War a village chieftain concocted a tale that Engelbrecht was supplying game flesh to a German gunboat that had been seen off the coast of Yala. He was imprisoned again, and though eventually released, he never regained his job. He died in poverty near Wirawila in 1926. We saw a herd of wild cattle that were descendants of Engelbrecht's original domestic

H.H. Engelbrecht, the first warden of the Yala National Park. He was fearless, obstinate – and widely hated.

Almost as soon as we entered Yala's arid and sandy terrain we saw spotted deer.

herd, which had scattered across Yala when he was in the detention camp.

In his memoirs Leonard Woolf tells a story that reveals a lot about the strength of both Engelbrecht and leopards. Woolf, Engelbrecht, and a young police superintendent named Hodson were out on a hunt in the Magampattu jungle. They were walking in single file near some rocks when a leopard appeared about twenty-five yards away. Hodson shot at and hit it, but it staggered off. The hunters followed a trail of blood up onto the rocks and into a cave, whose entrance was partially blocked by a boulder.

"A wounded leopard is one of the most dangerous of all animals, and to follow him into a dark cave is sheer madness, as Engelbrecht knew even better than I," Woolf wrote. At first the men could see nothing in the cave, but when their eyes grew accustomed to the semi-darkness they both saw the tail of the leopard protruding from behind the boulder. Englebrecht fired at the tail to make the leopard move and give Woolf a chance to shoot, but the cat only growled. Engelbrecht then cut down a sapling and said that he would climb on to the boulder and poke the leopard out with the sapling so that Woolf could get a shot at it. Woolf protested that this was madness, but Engelbrecht pointed out that they could not leave it now. Woolf "feebly gave way," as he put it. With them were three game watchers, and at this point Woolf suddenly caught sight of them, each perched on the top of a small tree, looking down upon him and Engelbrecht with horror. "The sight did not reassure me," Woolf admitted, before going on to finish the story:

> Engelbrecht climbed on to the boulder: he was unarmed and he knew that I was about the worst shot with a rifle in the world. But he poked down at the leopard. At first there was only a burst of savage growls, and then suddenly the leopard sprang into view. I could see him quite clearly sitting up, slightly sideways, three or four yards inside the cave. I fired and jumped aside to the left in front of the boulder and Engelbrecht, Hodson, and I cowered down pressed together in the narrow space away from the opening. When I fired the whole cave was filled with smoke and out of the smoke a foot or two from us whizzed the leopard turning head over heels. He fell upon the rocks below, turned another somersault round another boulder, and there again was the end of his tail jutting out beyond the rock. Very, very cautiously we crept down with our rifles ready and peered round the rock. He was dead; by a complete fluke, which I don't think I should have succeeded in bringing off once in twenty times, I had shot him through the heart.

The Ceylon green bee-eater, one of the island's most colourful birds, is seen everywhere in the lowlands.

The Talgasmankada lodge in Yala is a small bungalow, just a couple of rooms and an L-shaped veranda, on the bank of the Menik River. Its name means "the crossing where the thal trees are." The lodge was almost bare of furnishings and had no electricity and only a little water, but it was wonderfully shaded by huge deciduous trees. Colombo, not to mention London or Toronto, seemed a universe away. The curry at lunch was especially tasty, the bathe in the river especially refreshing, and all afternoon we eased ourselves into the rhythms of the jungle.

Almost immediately I felt the joy of having freedom at last. The only telephone connection, when it worked, was from Tissamaharama, forty miles away. We had to go there every few days for fresh food, and I used to call Gillian in Colombo to assure her that we were all right. Other than that, news of fighting in the area or reports of murders reached us only by word of mouth. At last I began to clear my mind, to the point where I cared only if I had a pair of dry shoes, comfortable clothes, a hat against the sun, and a dose of mosquito repellent.

Except for the leopards, of course. I had to see and photograph the leopards. It was a fixation that drove me. After all, I had come to Yala for little other reason than that. What if I spent two weeks here and didn't see one? As in Africa, this anxiety produced what we called "leopard fever" after a few days. Right from the moment I stepped from the jeep I was seized by this ambition. I spent time that first afternoon practising with my camera, trying different lenses, different films, different lights, for the moment I saw a leopard. In sunlight or shade, at noon or dusk, standing still or on the run, I had to be ready to bang off a shot with confidence.

In fact, I wanted to get past the sighting and the shot as quickly as possible, so that I could relax with the leopards. I wanted to become familiar with them, to observe their movements, to know their habits, to research their relationship with humans, as part of my obsession with the man-eater of Punanai. But first I had to see them, of course, and I managed to infuse Childers and Lucky with my own impatience.

No leopard the first afternoon, not even any tracks. Herds of deer, buffalo mating, huge wild boar, brilliant birds. But no leopard.

Until that night. We were sleeping out on the veranda. The rooms were too hot, so a row of cots had been placed along the gallery facing the river. I noticed

Wanni Arachi, one of our trackers. He is known to have foiled a leopard's nighttime attack on one of the staff in a Yala park bungalow.

that Lucky and Childers chose the cots in the centre, and our driver, Raja, took the one farthest from the opening, leaving me with the first bed a wild animal would come to on its nocturnal prowl. Despite the angry cries of the peacocks, I slept well. The day had been long; I was content to be back to the magical nights and the remembered smell of the kerosene lamps. The breeze was cool, and there were no mosquitoes. From time to time I was awakened by a sound and shone my flashlight into the eerie blackness, catching the inquisitive eyes of deer and hares and squirrels. But I slept through the rasping, sawing sound of a leopard. Wanni Arachi, our park tracker, heard it coming from across the river several times during the night.

"One hot night a leopard came into my room and lay down on the bed beside me," Anna Kavan wrote in a short fiction called "The Visit."

I was half asleep, and did not realize at first that it was a leopard. I seemed to be dreaming the sound of some large, soft-footed creature padding quietly through the house, the doors of which were wide open because of the intense heat. It was almost too dark to see the lithe, muscular shape coming into my room treading softly on velvet paws, coming straight to the bed without hesitation, as if perfectly familiar with its position.

A light spring, then warm breath on my arm, on my neck and shoulder, as the visitor sniffed me before lying down. It was not until later, when moonlight entering through the window revealed an abstract spotted design, that I recognized the form of an unusually large, handsome leopard stretched out beside me.

His breathing was deep though almost inaudible. He seemed to be sound asleep. I watched the regular contractions and expansions of the deep chest, admired the elegant relaxed body and supple limbs, and was confirmed in my conviction that the leopard is the most beautiful of all wild animals....While I observed him, I was all the time breathing his natural odor, a wild primeval smell of sunshine, freedom, moon and crushed leaves, combined with the cool freshness of the spotted hide, still damp with the midnight moisture of jungle plants. I found his non-human scent, surrounding him like an aura of strangeness, peculiarly attractive and stimulating.

My bed, like the walls of the house, was made of palm-leaf matting stretched over short bamboos, smooth and cool to the touch, even in the great heat. It was not so much a bed as a room within a room, an open staging about twelve feet

A wounded leopard is one of the most dangerous of all animals. To follow one into a cave is sheer madness.

square, so there was ample space for the leopard as well as myself. I slept better that night than I had since the hot weather started, and he too seemed to sleep peacefully at my side.

The close proximity of this powerful body of another species gave me a pleasant sensation that I am at a loss to name.

When I awoke in the faint light of dawn, with the parrots screeching outside, he had already got up and left the room.

However restless the night, I was always anxious to get up well before dawn, and I was seldom tired. One of the servants would light the lamps, so that we wouldn't bump into walls or one another as we made our way to wash and shave. Then a cup of strong instant coffee and a sweet banana, and we were off – though not before wiping the jeep's seats of the thick dew that had settled on them.

It was a special time of day, cool, fragrant, silent, as our sleepy eyes strained to catch a leopard's movement in the headlights. The damp breeze helped to wake us, though it was never chilly enough to make us wear sweaters. We would drive for a couple of hours, stopping periodically to listen for leopards or deer, pausing to photograph the buffalo or sambur against the spectacular sunrise, admiring the golden glow spreading across the land. The gold became an intense yellow and the breeze became a shimmering heat. This was always a good hour to see game. Then we would pull under the shade of a tree to have breakfast – sweet tea, chick peas, and a spicy mixture of coconut and chillies. It rarely lasted more than fifteen minutes, before we would push on till noon down the dusty roads.

Out in the jeep we found more deer, more birds, a small crocodile basking in the sun at the edge of a pool, an elephant, and more wild buffalo. The elephant and the buffalo seemed less dangerous than their cousins whom I had seen in Africa, but both have been known to kill humans. In 1974 a Japanese Buddhist monk visited Magulmahavihara on the outskirts of Yala at dusk and, despite being warned by the staff, decided to proceed with his pilgrimage into the night. Two days later his body was found. He had been killed by an elephant, and his body had been ravaged by jackals.

Though he was sixty years old, our tracker, Wanni Arachi, proved to have

Anver, another park tracker – invaluable for his keen eyesight and sensitive hearing.

amazing eyes for animals and birds. He seemed to spot everything effortlessly. The only evidence of leopard, however, turned out to be a few old paw marks along the sandy road.

We returned to the lodge for a lunch of fish curry made from jackfish that had been dried in the sun for a couple of days. The dehydrated flesh was tough and salty on its own, but delicious when mixed with rice and vegetables. It's a favourite dish among Sri Lankans, and all along the coast I had seen the fish being dried beside houses and huts.

The afternoon was disappointing, except for plenty of elephants, including one full-grown tusker having an evening drink. Later, I walked beside the river, enjoying a remarkably vivid sunset and reacquainting myself with some of the birds I had known as a child: jungle fowl, serpent eagles, Indian snake-darters, paradise flycatchers, Brahminy kites, sea eagles, and a flock of pelicans.

We slept again on the veranda that night, but with less success. There were louder and more disturbing jungle noises, and neither Childers nor Lucky seemed able to settle down. Deep in the night, a shot rang out. It came from the other side of the river, perhaps a mile away. Terrorists? I knew the others were awake, but nobody moved or said anything. The sharp crack of the rifle set off a frenzied chorus of shrieks, led by the peacocks and a couple of langurs, and amidst them came a blood-curdling scream. It sounded like a child being strangled. I lay tense and wide awake until the commotion quietened down and I was able to drop off to sleep.

I used to go snipe-shooting with my father early in the morning, and he taught me to use a twelve-bore. "You have to keep it cocked and at the ready," he said, "because the birds will fly up right in front of you with a great purring noise. They'll be moving quickly and soon out of range, so you'll have to learn to put the gun to your shoulder and immediately bang away." We walked in our rubber boots through the paddy fields. Sure enough, a snipe flew up rapidly. My father hoisted his gun and shot, but he missed. "You see, they're very difficult," he said. We walked another hundred yards. Suddenly, almost at my feet, there was a purring sound, and a snipe took off away from me. I pulled my trigger without lifting the gun from my waist, and the bird fell dead.

"How on earth did you do that?" my father asked incredulously. He was really upset. "That's not the way it's done."

In fact, it seems, I had shot into the water and a couple of bullets had ricocheted

The crested hawk eagle may be the legendary "devil bird" – an omen of death, according to local superstition.

up into the bird. My father, who was a good shot, wasn't sure whether to be proud or disgusted at my accomplishment.

It's the same when I take photographs, particularly of wildlife. I tend to bang away quickly, rather than wait for quality and drama, because I don't want to take the risk of getting no picture at all. This usually bothers professional photographers, who prefer patience and slow movements, but sometimes my imperious way reaps better dividends.

The next morning Wanni Arachi told us the gurgled scream had come from the "devil bird." It's rarely seen, and there is still a debate about what it is. Suggestions include a brown wood owl and a crested honey buzzard, but the best evidence, amassed in 1968 by Dr. R.L. Spittel, an old friend of the Ondaatje family, suggests it is either the crested hawk eagle or the forest eagle owl. Whatever its identity, there is a local superstition that the devil bird is an omen of death.

According to the ancient legend, once there was a jealous husband who suspected his wife of infidelity. During her absence he murdered their child and made a curry from the corpse. He served it to his wife, who ate it until she found the baby's finger on her plate. Mad with grief and disgust, she fled into the jungle and killed herself, but the gods transformed her into a bird, the devil bird, which still horrifies the world with the woman's hysterical screams.

The cry has also been compared to the sound of a baby being strangled, a boy being tortured, and a lost child whose wailings break off into a pitiful, choking sob. Dr. Spittel found a variation of the myth in the folklore of the Veddas, the island's earliest inhabitants: "A Vedda and his son Koa were out hunting for three days without success. They were both very hungry. The father told his son to kindle a fire and, when it was aflame, thrust his son Koa into it and roasted him and ate some of his flesh. He took part of it to his wife, who cooked it and was sharing it out when she suddenly became aware that it was her son's flesh. Digging the handle of the spoon into her head, she screamed, 'Koa,' fled into the forest and died. And now as the crested *ulama* she makes the midnight jungle echo with that wail."

Even stranger are the tragic tales told by a man named Shelley Crozier, who went hunting on three occasions in the 1920s with three different friends to the same waterhole in the remote Eastern Province. Each time he heard the devil bird cry under a full moon. The first time was with his friend Phillip, like Crozier a special apprentice with the railway.

"Here was a whitish brown bird with a hooked beak and about the size of a hawk, craning its neck to get a better look at us," Crozier reported. "When exactly opposite my friend, it stretched its neck forward, puffed its neck feathers out and then shattered the silence with its deadly scream. Screaming and shaking its head up and down, as though he was abusing my friend, he shut up and was about to fly off when I shot it a bare foot away from the point of my gun. My friend was sweating from every pore of his body, and by the light of the moon, he looked as pale as death."

"I am not long for this world," Phillip prophesied. Then, at dawn, seeing the dead bird, he shouted, "For God's sake take me from here." Five days later Phillip was struck by a bus. "The curse of the devil bird," he said to Crozier in the hospital, and died.

The next year, Crozier visited the same place, with another friend. They heard the horrible scream and the bird flew out of the night and dropped a chameleon onto the friend's lap. He laughed it off, but four days later he became ill and was sent to the hospital. "Devil bird," he whispered to Crozier, and died.

The next year in the same place, Crozier was with yet another friend, Noel. Noel, too, had been warned, but insisted on making the trip. "Devil or angel, I stay," Noel said bravely at first. But as the darkness came, his courage departed. "Let's can this damn shoot and get out of here, even if we have to get lost!" he said. But they didn't go, nor did they sleep. Then the scream. "I am bloody sorry I came," Noel said. An hour later another scream, and the bird flew low over Noel's head. Two weeks later he was dead.

Rather belatedly, Crozier decided not to tempt fate any further, stating: "I vowed that I would never again take a friend to that place as long as I lived."

The morning brought a change of plan that seemed another ill omen. Originally we were intending to spend five days in Talgasmankada, go off to another part of the park for a while, then return for five more days. Now, instead of returning, we would go on to the Patanangala bungalow on the coast. Childers explained that this was to allow him to pursue his research about turtles, but I suspected that he and Lucky were protecting me from danger. The Talgasmankada lodge had been burned to the ground a couple of years before, and it was on the main escape route for terrorists trying to flee north into the interior from the coast. The fighting was getting closer, and Childers thought it best for us to move on.

Forget about devil birds and terrorists. I was more interested in the pursuit of leopards. I had everyone in the jeep and on the track by sunrise, and we spent every hour of the morning going up and down every track in the area. It was strenuous and exhilarating, but we had no luck. Shortly before noon we gave up and drove to the park's office to pick up some "mutton," as they call goat meat. While there we were asked to give another tracker, S.M. "Anver" Anverdeen, a ride over to his assignment at a fishing camp, and we agreed.

"We'll cut off your ears if you don't find us a leopard on the way," Childers joked.

As it happened, Anver knew a trick or two. Leopards have a habit of marking their territory in fairly regular patterns, but they never cross in front of a jeep. They wait for the jeep to pass, then they continue on their route. So, while the rest of us were staring ahead and to the side, Anver was constantly looking back. Suddenly he grabbed me firmly and spun me around, and there on the road was a leopard ambling behind and away out of our dust.

I was thrilled. The jeep circled round and followed the cat as closely as possible. It was a male, much bigger than any I had seen in Africa, and tawnier in colour, and it was plodding purposefully through the scrub. I managed to get a few photographs before it disappeared into the brush. We tracked its marks to a kill it had dropped near the road, and then we came across a second leopard, a female straddling the branch of a pallu tree. The sky had become too cloudy for a really clear shot, but I felt an enormous excitement. I had found my Sri Lankan leopard, the island's dominant beast, the one without peer.

In 1951, the year I was taken out of school, I went to work in London at the National Bank of India. I was seventeen years old and no longer a rich boy with the world at my feet. Instead, I was thrown into another mystifying and rather intimidating environment where I began with no idea about what to do. I was assigned to go through documents and bills and invoices, without ever really understanding how all these pieces fitted into the grand scheme. I was shoved around from department to department for five years.

As at Blundell's, cricket served me better than work. I began playing cricket for the bank and then for the United Banks, and I eventually drew praise from the chairman of the board. I was a kind of star again, though only a trainee, and I acquired British ambitions as well as British methods. My aspirations were relatively modest at first – to work at the bank for a few years and return to Ceylon as its senior person there – but by the time I was offered the position of assistant manager in Colombo in 1956, I had already set my sights much higher.

Sri Lankan leopards are much bigger than any I had seen in Africa, and tawnier in colour.

There didn't seem to be much opportunity for entrepreneurs in the England of the early 1950s, and Ceylon was experiencing great difficulties in the aftermath of its independence. I could see that an era was ending, the era of British rule. Taking what was in fact my first major investment decision, I compared the gross national products of the industrialized world and concluded that Britain was on the decline. I wouldn't stay in London or go back with one of the British banks; I would emigrate to Canada.

My mother was shocked, my uncle was horrified, my father said nothing, but it didn't really matter. I had been forced to become independent, and now independence seemed strangely invigorating. I was determined to make my own decisions without depending on anyone else. After Blundell's and the bank, I was ready to start all over again.

A buffalo giving birth as other females crowd around to protect her calf from the jungle crows.

I have always identified with predators. I didn't set out to become a predator in the world of business, though I was one in a manner of speaking. Not that I've killed people, but I have had to be strong and tough. In business, as in the jungle, one is either predator or prey; and since I didn't want to be prey, I had to get power. Power isn't a case of bossing people around. It's a case of controlling the territory. That's what the English did when they controlled Ceylon. That's what the Tamil Tigers were trying to do. That's what leopards do all the time. And, though I am cautious enough not to become a victim, that's the power that I walked away from in business. Now I was in new territory, someone else's territory, leopard country. There were new rules, and I had to learn them to survive.

For almost forty years I cut my way through the jungle of corporate finance. Once I understood the banking business, I moved to stockbroking. As soon as I arrived in Canada, I taught myself the game, the players, the companies, what made the companies tick, the political context, the personalities of the owners, everything that could help me master the field. I broadened my knowledge, I developed my contacts, I worked hard, until every part of my brain and every sinew of my body seemed trained to do this one thing – finance – extremely well. Doing what I was best at doing, I just had to apply myself and my time in order to succeed. I went from dealing in pieces of paper for others to dealing in pieces of paper for myself – somewhat as my grandfather had done with land – and then I started dealing for my own companies. What could have been an enormous failure became an enormous success. It was a slow, cautious, methodical, opportunistic growth, but it became fantastic.

My grandmother Lalla was an inveterate gambler. She hated playing even simple card games like whist or snap if we didn't gamble. "It's absolutely ridiculous not to play cards for money," she would say, giving us some coins to compete for. As children we didn't take this very seriously, of course, but years later I remembered some of her lessons about risk: how to bluff, how to push people to their limit, how to appear to have more than you actually have, how to play fast, and – most important of all – how to be anxious to get on with the game and win.

We got back to the Talgasmankada bungalow around noon, to rest, wash off the red dust of the morning, and have a proper lunch. The rice and curry were usually so tasty that I had trouble not overeating or, as a result, getting drowsy. The others seemed to want a tropical siesta, but I was eager to go out again after three-quarters of an hour. My experience in Africa had taught me that if you want to see game you have to cover ground. You make your own breaks. The harder you work, the more you see, so we tended to work hard, even in the worst heat of the day (always equipped with hats against the sun and dark glasses against the glare). It paid off. We saw leopards twice in the afternoon, as they sought their own respite from the heat by lying up in trees. In the end, we probably saw a dozen different leopards on eighteen occasions, but only because we worked hard and covered a lot of ground.

We saw a buffalo giving birth, as other females crowded around her as protection from the jungle crows, but even that amazing and moving sight couldn't alleviate my frustration at not sighting, once again, the leopards we had seen before lunch.

We usually got back to the bungalow soon after dark, about seven in the evening. After a quick wash, we would have dinner – a slightly more formal affair than lunch, with frequent company and good conversation. (There was only one terrible meal, when, for my benefit, the cook attempted roast chicken in the English fashion. I advised against a repeat performance, and after that we stuck happily to our meat, fish, and vegetable curries.) Sometimes we would talk after dinner, or I would interview local villagers about leopards, but usually we were ready for bed quite soon after dinner.

We went to bed relatively early, around nine o'clock, after the nightly ritual of rubbing ourselves all over with citronella oil to ward off the mosquitoes. Once the kerosene lamps were extinguished, the darkness was absolute. You could not see your toes without a flashlight, which each of us kept by his bed for going to the lavatory or investigating night sounds if they got too close. The nights were always restless. I never slept very well or very deeply, what with the heat, the insects, animal noises, human movements, or my nervous state. I seemed on constant alert, and four o'clock came as a relief.

Childers Jayawardhana, a former warden at Yala, had the cool, calm manner of a true naturalist.

However, that evening we had celebrated our morning's success with a wonderful drink, a mixture of thambili, the thirst-quenching water from the king coconut, and six-year-old arrack, the local alcohol, which is made by tapping the sap from an unopened coconut flower and fermenting it. The spiked thambili put me into a very deep sleep. The night was strangely quiet, too, so quiet that everyone commented on it the next day.

At dawn the next morning we practically walked into a large male leopard!

He was lying on the track less than a quarter of a mile from the lodge. He ran into the thorny thicket at once and we never saw him again, though we could hear his deep, guttural sawing for a long while. Later, about eleven miles away, where we had seen the leopards the day before, there were only the tracks of a crocodile. Presumably it had made its journey in the night to feed on what the cats had killed.

For much of the afternoon we stalked a female leopard we had spotted in the scrub, hiding from the sweltering sun. She kept slipping in and out of view, as if she had cubs behind the rock on which she had been sitting. Wanting to test the theory that a cornered leopard will attack only if it catches your eye, I approached her, looking through the lens of my camera. She was nervous and quickly hid behind the rock again, though I did manage to get a few pictures of her face.

In 1951 my mother moved to London and ran a boarding house, where I lived for a while. It was a humble job for someone raised in an imperial outpost and accustomed to servants and idle times, but she was better off in England. She had me and my sister Janet there, she was away from the ignominy and scandal of my father's troubles, and she became the centre of a wide circle of family and friends who sought her out for her fun and warmth. I thought the world of her, and we shared the spirit of picking ourselves up from the bottom. Happily, before she died in 1974, she was able to live comfortably in a Chelsea flat, where I visited her often on my increasingly frequent business trips between Toronto and London.

For much of the afternoon we stalked a female leopard. She kept slipping in and out of view, as if she had cubs behind the rock on which she had been sitting.

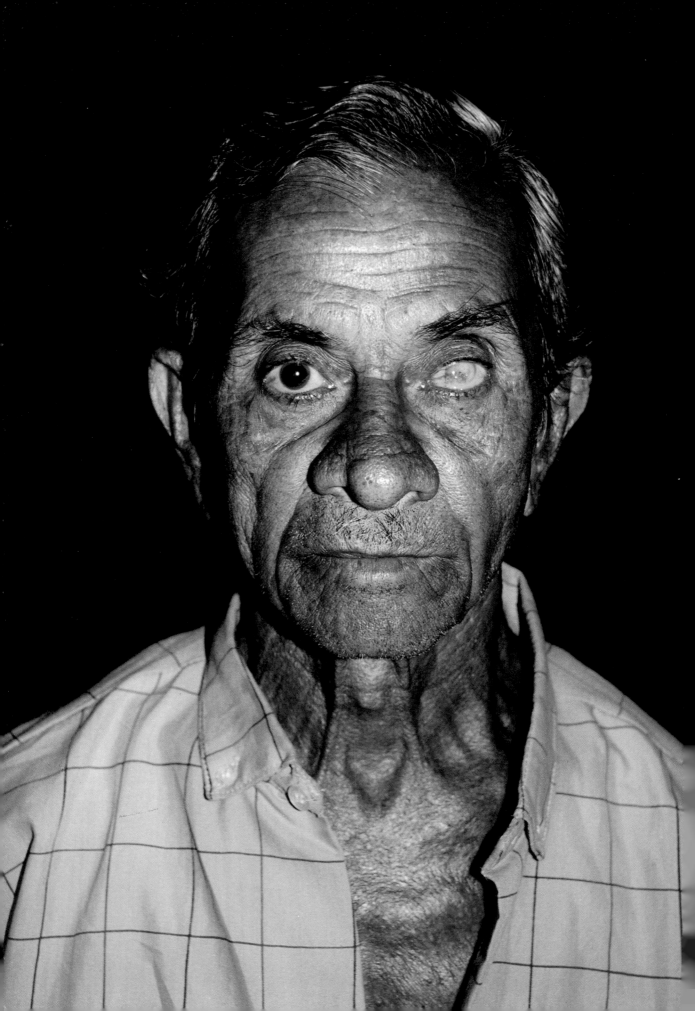

I met Shirley Perera, the assistant director of wildlife in charge of the south-east area. Apart from being the local boss of Yala, an avid bird enthusiast and bird-egg collector, and a very gentle and courteous human being, he was an excellent source of information. Everything seemed to get to him first. He told us that a new branch of the Tamil National Army had been created in the area, made up apparently of local Tamils and trained by the Indian soldiers who had been on the island as peace-keepers. This force was engaged in skirmishes with the Tamil Tigers for control of the coastal town of Kumana. Fighting between the two Tamil factions had broken out two weeks before only thirty miles from our bungalow.

In the evening Childers showed up with an old man named Baba Singho, a retired tracker from the village of Kumana. About seventy-five years old and blind in his left eye, he was rumoured to be the illegitimate grandson of the park's founder, H.H. Engelbrecht. Baba always aggressively denied the rumour, but he was certainly more fair-skinned than everyone else, and Leonard Woolf in his duties as district commissioner had found Engelbrecht responsible in at least one paternity case. Perhaps Baba Singho didn't want to be associated with a man who had been feared and despised by the natives. Kumana, also one of the most famous bird sanctuaries in the world, is the only village within the park, and its proud people seem to exist apart from other Sri Lankans, both because of their isolation, and because of their history as Sinhalese who had fled from the north during the rebellions of 1815.

I welcomed the chance to quiz the man about the habits of leopards, particularly man-eating leopards. He told us that elephants and full-grown buffalo are the only animals in Sri Lanka that have no cause to fear the leopard. Cattle, dogs, birds, and sometimes even humans are prey. Though the man-eater of Punanai is the only recorded case of a true man-eater, there are countless stories of others. Every year, for example, forty-five days before the July full moon, Hindu pilgrims set out from Jaffna in the north to journey three hundred miles to the shrine at Kataragama, some twenty-five miles from Yala. Many of them tire, get sick, and are left by the wayside. Their bodies, when found, appear mauled or mangled. It is unclear whether the leopards actually killed them or merely feasted on their corpses, but the pilgrims certainly believe they are in danger of being attacked while on the sacred journey.

Baba Singho, a retired tracker from the village of Kumana, told us countless stories of man-eating leopards. Only elephants and full-grown buffalo have no cause to fear the leopard.

As Childers translated for me, Baba insisted that some pilgrims had been attacked by leopards. In dramatic tones and with hand gestures for emphasis, he told of the time an uncle of his, an official of the Game Protection Society in the park's early years, came across a woman's corpse that had been mauled in such a way as to suggest that a leopard had killed her. The incident was memorable because her baby was found crying at her side, unharmed.

Pilgrims to Kataragama passed through Kumana, thus giving local leopards plenty of opportunity to acquire a taste for human flesh, which is supposed to have a "salty sweet" flavour. As a result, the villagers of Kumana had come to live in terror of man-eaters.

Never follow a wounded leopard, Baba warned us. A friend of his, another tracker, once wounded one. The animal ran off, but the next morning when the tracker was walking to his paddy fields, it leapt out and mauled his neck and shoulder. The villagers were convinced that it had lain in wait for him, vicious for vengeance.

Childers followed up with a leopard story of his own. Several years earlier a leopard was injured by a wild boar and took refuge in an abandoned bungalow within the park. The game ranger tried to coax it out, unsuccessfully. He then climbed onto the roof, removed some tiles, and tried to encourage the animal out the door that way. Instead, the leopard sprang upwards towards him, and its paw actually struck the rafter about fifteen feet above the floor. An amazing feat for a wounded animal, and another warning of how dangerous a cornered leopard can be.

Bathers by the roadside—very much part of everyday Sri Lankan life.

Leopards are both unpredictable and vindictive. They will kill for the sake of killing, and when they attack, they hurt. Those who have been mauled by lions and leopards say that a lion mauls both out of fear and in self-defence, whereas a leopard mauls to inflict pain. There is an evil and vicious streak in leopards that seems astonishing, given how beautiful they are.

My father was a big man, a giant of a man. His huge frame was always immaculately dressed. Even roaming around the estate in the heat, he wore neatly pressed shorts and knee socks. I often accompanied him then, because it was easy to follow the twinkle in his eyes and the enthusiasm in his voice – the very qualities that had made him such a good salesman and friend.

Though he always had my best interests at heart and encouraged me to pursue any passion, he could be strict, even brutal, if he saw me doing the wrong thing. Often his sharp criticisms hurt me more than he knew, but he had grown up never having to be diplomatic or sensitive. Whether at home in front of his children or at dinner with friends, he tended to speak his mind without really worrying about the consequences.

He liked everything to be in order, a reflection of his own neat style. He instinctively noticed when anything had been moved in a room and always asked why. This was part of his being in charge, at the helm, and everyone viewed him with a mixture of awe and fear. In his darkest moods, his character became very strange. These times could be quite terrifying, because we never understood what was happening or when it would end. Suddenly, everything simply went wrong. His control, his order, his love, his charisma – nothing worked anymore. As a family we were in disarray, waiting for the dawn, and praying that it would come soon.

All the talk about pilgrims got me curious, so the next morning we went to the Hindu shrine at Kataragama, eleven miles northeast of Tissamaharama. The path that had brought pilgrims of all faiths through the jungle for hundreds of years was now a highway, but thousands still walk the route through "God's country," chanting "Haro Hara." They come each year to ask for favours and blessings from the god Skanda. Like them, we took off our shoes in the village and went barefoot along the bank of the Menik River to a bridge. Below it dozens of pilgrims were bathing as ritual preparation for their ascent into the shrine, while women washed their clothes and children sported in the water.

Climbing up the long, straight, and pebbly path, I was aware of how important this visit was for Lucky. He hadn't been here for many years, he was very concerned about our safety, and he wanted to make vows in exchange for God Skanda's protection. We were silent, serious, and intent, even though I was hobbling from walking barefoot on the stones. The last stretch was lined with vendors selling incense and flowers, which we bought and took as offerings into the shrine. It was a simple white building rather than an ornate temple, and about a hundred worshippers were crowded into it. As we burned the joss sticks in homage to the deity, I too was overwhelmed by religious feeling. However awkward I felt, however out of place I looked among the devotees, I shared their involvement and their confidence for a moment. "Let me get home alive," I prayed, "and I will return some day to do something to help Sri Lanka."

There is a tradition that if you dash a coconut onto a concrete slab near the temple exit and the coconut splits cleanly down the middle your wish will be granted. I threw, and my coconut cracked into two perfect halves.

On our way back to the lodge at the end of the day, we saw a large male leopard walking away from us into the night.

I never saw my father again after I left Ceylon to go to school in England. Once he lost everything – his family as well as his money – he retreated to Rock Hill, which had been my grandfather's coconut estate near Kegalle. It wasn't a huge property and the house wasn't very grand, but when we went there every Christmas as children the place seemed remote and immense. My father lived out his last years there, farming, drinking, selling off chunk after chunk of land to make ends meet; and though he remarried and had another child, I used to think of him as lonely and depressed. If I felt badly about our loss of status and pride, how much worse must he have felt? He had been responsible; he had stayed behind to face the music; he had experienced the slide from the top of the heap; he had heard the gossip and seen the looks of reproach. Occasionally he answered my letters, but he never opened his soul, except once on a Christmas card, when he said that he missed his family and the best years of his life.

My father died a shattered man, shattered in mind and body, screaming at his second wife, searching for a hidden bottle of gin, and smashing his head on a stone floor. Five people had carried his heavy body to the car and rushed it to the hospital in Kegalle, but nobody could have saved him. In fact, he had been beyond saving for many years, lost to everyone who held him dear. His mind had shut out the world around him, a world he neither wanted nor understood. But he went on living – even after his actual death – as the most powerful influence on the lives of his children.

In 1965, while I was walking down Bay Street in Toronto's financial district, someone brought me the news that had been cabled to the office: my father had died. He was sixty-one years old. His death hurt, of course, but it also served as another kick to my ambition. "Now it's you," I said to myself. "You're the head of the family. Everybody else is looking to you, nobody else but you, and you're the one who's going to make it or break it."

"If a devil has entered a man, and is harming him, and taking his life from him, the man should make a vow to the god, so my father used to say," explains a character in Leonard Woolf's novel *The Village in the Jungle*. "Then he should go to the temple at Beragama at the time of the great festival, and roll in the dust round the temple three times every day, and call upon the god in a loud voice to free him from the devil. And perhaps, if he calls loud enough, the god will hear him and order the devil to leave him. Then the devil will be afraid of the god's power, and will leave the man, who will be freed from the evil."

That night I learned that the JVP had burned down one of the park's luxury bungalows only a short time before we got there. It had been built to accommodate government VIPs and foreign dignitaries, and had caused some resentment locally. That news, and too much tamarind in the goat curry at dinner, wouldn't let me get to sleep.

We followed a male leopard near the bungalow before dawn, but even the jeep's headlights didn't provide enough light for a photograph. Later there was a female resting in the sand by the side of the track, but she was very skittish and disappeared quickly.

Pilgrims washing in the Menik River near Kataragama.

When my mother gave up everything and had nothing, she went to England and started at the bottom with the zest and will of a real trouper. She almost revelled in her new role as a housekeeper in Chelsea in a rooming house, in which she and my sister Janet shared the basement and I had a tiny room in the attic. When the chips were down she got on her knees and scrubbed floors to keep her family together. Perhaps it was because she had earned her living before she was married, perhaps it was because of her tremendous personality, but I never heard her complain. Certainly my father could not have done the same thing, because all his life he had others to do everything for him.

My mother cleaned the rooms, looked after the laundry, provided breakfast every morning, and created a whole new family for herself. Even in poverty she was the star on her own stage. Many of her friends from Colombo came to visit, staying in the rooming house to be near her, and the place was always full of life. Despite her reduced circumstances, she instilled in us a pride and a sense of purpose that were infectious, and I was enormously proud of her.

Of course, we were still snobs. Though we'd been knocked off our perch as wealthy and pampered colonials, God help the person who treated us as inferiors. Indeed, we all put on a new front as extrovert bohemians who knew everyone and had a great time.

I really grew into adulthood then. Though I was just a teenager, my mother asked my advice the way she had asked for advice from my father, and we all began to realize that we were no longer his family. We were living in another world.

At the park's headquarters we heard about the two JVP rebels who had been captured near Tissamaharama, killed, and displayed from a roof as a warning. The locals seemed more relaxed about the threats than I was. Why worry, they said, as long as you don't make a target of yourself?

Lucky had a solution for my bad stomach: belli fruit. There was even a Sri Lankan rhyme about it.

Belli Kanakote Bada Yanawa
Bada Yanakote Belli Kanawa

Peacocks mating. In a few weeks the male will lose all his beautiful tail feathers, which will not grow back until it is time for next year's courting dance.

Loosely translated this means that the ubiquitous belli fruit is able to cure both diarrhoea and constipation.

At noon we moved to the Heenwewa bungalow, about fifteen miles inland to the west. It didn't have quite as idyllic a location as Talgasmankada, but it felt safer and had a pretty setting overlooking an ancient tank.

Over lunch Childers told me a story. Ten years earlier, the keeper of this bungalow had been sleeping on the veranda of his own quarters at the back when he felt something grabbing at his feet. He awoke with a start and saw a leopard at the end of his cot. He screamed, and Wanni, his tracker then, too, came rushing to his defence, armed only with a flashlight. The leopard took off, but remained only a short distance away.

"Leopards often live in remarkable proximity to man," Childers informed me.

Anver joined us for the next day's drive. He and Wanni had incredible eyes, sure instincts, and sharp ears. Often we stopped the jeep so they could just listen: for the agitated bark of a deer, for the irritated scoldings of a squirrel, for the throaty kako-kak of a grey langur, for the alarm cries of a bird. Years of living observantly in the wilderness had made them acutely aware of every signal around them. Anver promised we would see a leopard by the time the sun rose – and he was right.

We saw two, in fact, a male and a female sitting up on top of a rock. They were quite far away, but we inched closer. After forty-five minutes I was able to get a portrait of the male looking towards us and the morning sun. The subtle lemon light brought out his tawny splendour. We observed them at length, hoping to see them mate, but they moved off to a more secluded and shaded part of the rock.

I saw a peacock mating in the afternoon, after having exhibited his gorgeous feathers before no fewer than eight hens. He chose one, or did one choose him? Enjoy it, my friend, I thought, because soon those feathers of which you are so proud will fall off and you'll look no different from the females until the fall monsoon!

A jackal protecting its kill from ravenous jungle crows.

The Heenwewa bungalow keeper was said to have a rare talent: he could cure the bites of scorpions, snakes, and spiders. These creatures were a constant danger in Sri Lanka, and many of them could kill you.

Cobras, tick polongas, kraits, tarantula spiders – you always had to watch out for them. You didn't walk in tall grass, you didn't walk in bare feet, you shook out your shoes each morning in case a scorpion had made a cosy bed in one of them. (I once found a scorpion in my shoe on the Caribbean island of Barbuda, and I once was bitten by one in Africa, and neither shock was pleasant.) There were pythons, too, but they strangle rather than poison. On one of our drives I saw a python that a villager had captured, and for a lark and a photograph I had it wrapped around my neck. Even after an instant I had a hard time pulling it away from my throat.

Clouds to the east at dawn. No leopards on the rock. Terrorists near the Menik River. Terrific heat. Lots of birds, but few animals around the tank. Hours on rough roads. We passed a very young buffalo calf that had been killed by a leopard. Eight Ceylon jackals tore nervously at its small carcass. They kept looking at us and eventually hurried away. We hid on the other side of a stream, but only one jackal was brave enough to return. It was a funny kind of bravery, interrupted by flashes of real fear and desperate efforts to drive away a dozen large jungle crows.

The afternoon wasn't any better, though a family of elephants passed a few feet from the jeep, and we saw an evening kill by a crested hawk eagle.

We were back at the rock by sunrise, and we waited for the leopards. At last they came, the male and female, high on a ledge in the shadows. We kept absolutely silent. The sunlight shone gloriously on the promontory on which they were circling each other. Then they were gone. I hadn't much time, just a few moments of watching really, but I felt delirious with joy. Lucky, Childers, Wanni, and Anver looked relieved. The pressure was off.

Mating leopards high on a ledge in the morning light. After only a few moments they moved off to a more secluded and shaded part of the rock.

Content and relaxed, we took a break to do a little sightseeing at Situlpahuwa, one of two existing Buddhist shrines not far from the Heenwewa bungalow that date from the days of the Ruhuna kings in the first century B.C. (We also visited the other, the smaller, simpler, and earlier shrine at Magulmahavihara, where we found a sect of Buddhist nuns living in its caves.) It was a paltry testament to an ancient civilization whose leaders had created a mighty irrigation system, now given over to wildlife, and whose monks had meditated by the thousands all over the rich kingdom, now conquered by the jungle. Its golden era passed, a victim of war and drought and famine and malaria.

The buffalo bulls were becoming aggressively territorial; it was time to round up their herds for mating. The buffalo cows, too, were getting dangerously protective of their calves. The calves were especially vulnerable at this stage, easy prey for leopards. I photographed one young calf with a wound festering on its muzzle from a leopard's attack about two days before.

I was reminded of a tale told by Sir Samuel Baker in his book *Eight Years in Ceylon*, published in 1874. Baker is credited with developing the town of Nuwara Eliya. He was also one of the great adventurers who got to the source of the Nile, an expedition he made shortly after the epic journeys of Sir Richard Burton and Sir John Speke.

> About three years ago [Baker wrote] a leopard took it into his head to try the beef-steaks of a very savage and sharp-horned cow, who with her calf was the property of the blacksmith. It was a dark and rainy night, the blacksmith and his wife were in bed, and the cow and her calf were nestled in the warm straw in the cattle shed. The door was locked, and all was apparently secure, when the hungry leopard prowled stealthily round the cow house, sniffing the prey within. Strong smell of the leopard at once alarmed the keen senses of the cow, made doubly acute by her anxiety for her little charge, and she stood ready for the danger as the leopard having mounted on the roof commenced scratching his way through the thatch.
>
> Down he sprang! But at the same instant, with a splendid charge, the cow pinned him against the wall, and a battle ensued which can easily be imagined. A coolie slept in the corner of the cattle shed, whose wondering senses were completely scattered when he found himself the unwilling umpire of the fight.
>
> He rushed out and shut the door. In a few minutes he succeeded in awakening the blacksmith, who struck a light, and proceeded to load a pistol, the only weapon that he possessed. During the whole of this time the bellowing of the cow, the roars

Buddhist monks in the cave shelter at Magulmahavihara.

of the leopard, and the thumping, trampling which proceeded from the cattle shed, explained the savage nature of the fight.

The blacksmith, who was no sportsman, shortly found himself with a lanthorn in one hand, a pistol in the other, and no idea what he meant to do. He waited, therefore, at the cattle shed door, and holding the light so as to shine through the numerous small apertures in the shed, he looked in.

The leopard no longer prowled, but the cow was mad with fury. She alternately threw a large dark mass above her head, then quickly pinned it to the ground on its descent, then bored it against the wall as it crawled helplessly towards a corner of the shed. This was the "beefeater" in reduced circumstances! The gallant little cow had nearly killed him, and was giving him the finishing strokes. The blacksmith perceived the leopard's helpless state, and boldly opening the door he discharged his pistol, and the next moment was bolting as hard as he could run with the war-like cow after him. She was regularly "up" and was ready for anything or anybody. However, she was at length pacified, and the dying leopard was put out of his misery.

On the way to Tissa for supplies we saw three leopards on the rock. Another male had joined the pair. The sun had barely risen, and though we took almost an hour to approach quietly, they quickly slunk away.

En route we gave an old man a lift. One moonless night, he told us, he was sitting outside his house when he heard one of his calves bleating in distress. He called for his wife to bring his flashlight, and there in its glare saw a leopard holding the calf by its muzzle. The old man grabbed a pole made of weera wood, a very hard wood, and stunned the leopard with a blow to the head. Then he killed it. The fascinating thing was that, despite the man's charge, the cat wouldn't run from its prey.

I saw a newspaper in Tissa, with more reports of trouble in the area. "Foodstuffs in trawlers for TNA cadres in Kumana?" asked one of the headlines. About three hundred Tamil National Army cadres were reported to be in several camps in Kumana, just twenty-three miles from Yala, surrounded by rival cadres of Tamil Tigers. The villagers caught between the two factions were said to be running out of food and confined to their houses, by order of the Tigers. A skirmish seemed inevitable.

The leopard is territorial and tends to be the least nocturnal of all the cats, though difficult to spot in the shade during the heat of the day. Its senses of sound and sight are extraordinarily keen, but it has almost no sense of smell. It's an intelligent animal. When a shot is fired, for example, a leopard often appears, having learned that a shot usually means a kill. And when hunting for monkeys, a leopard will often just claw or leap at the base of the tree, knowing that terror alone often makes a monkey miss its jump and fall to the ground. In the same way a leopard will use its guttural roar to locate deer. The roar causes the deer to bark in panic, thus revealing their whereabouts.

My father was a snob, and he didn't like me fraternizing with the servants. Their quarters were out of bounds to his children. One day he caught me there and gave me a hard slap. The impact of his signet ring left a bruise on my cheek that lasted for days.

And then there was the day when I was with Gopal, the house boy, who was teaching me about charms and black magic. I had been fascinated as a boy by the idea of magic spells, ever since I had discovered that they were practised widely in Ceylon. There were a great number of charmers in the area, capable of casting spells that would bring sickness and even death, not just on one person but on entire families. Wives would be made to leave their husbands; men would be compelled to follow the women who desired them; children would rise up against their parents; and a village would be plunged into hardship by the devastation of its crops. As a result, people carried counter-charms around their necks or as amulets. Even now, with modernization, black magic is present on the island in a quiet but pervasive way. I have been told of many instances where sick people, unable to be cured by their doctors, have been healed by the lifting of a curse.

Though I was born and remain a Christian, I have been convinced of the power of witchery. A doctor once told me that his brother, a government officer whose legs were crippled, had been cured when one of these spells had been lifted. And often when I was young I heard similar stories about mental power and sorcery from the servants. Whenever my father caught me learning these superstitions, I received a beating.

Late in the afternoon, as the sun was almost setting, we spotted a large male leopard out hunting. Though we were only thirty yards from him, he didn't seem concerned about us. He was constantly yawning, a sure sign of hunger, and he was concentrating on his prey: two small buffalo calves protected by a herd of females, tough and dangerous adversaries. The leopard crouched beneath a tree near the water hole where the buffalo were drinking.

"I have seen a full-grown bullock with its neck broken by a leopard," Samuel Baker reported:

> It is the popular belief that the effect is produced by a blow of the paw; this is not the case; it is not simply the blow, but it is the combination of the weight, muscular power, and the momentum of the spring, which rendered the effects of a leopard's attack so surprising.
>
> Few leopards rush boldly upon their prey like a dog; they stalk their game, and advance crouchingly, making use of every object that will afford them cover until they are within a few bounds of their victim. Then the immense power of muscle is displayed in the concentrated energy of the spring; he flies through the air, and settles on the throat, usually throwing his own body over the animal, while his teeth and claws are fixed on the neck: this is the manner in which the spine of an animal is broken, by a sudden twist, and not simply a blow.
>
> The blow from the paw is nevertheless immensely powerful, and at one stroke will rip open a bullock like a knife; but the aftereffects of the wound are still more to be dreaded than the force of the stroke. There is a peculiar poison in the claw, which is highly dangerous. This is caused by the putrid flesh which they are constantly tearing, and which is apt to cause gangrene by innoculation.

The leopard we were watching didn't move a muscle for twenty minutes. Then, just as the light faded, he moved silently downwind and disappeared into the long grass. Though we had had an excellent opportunity to observe his strategy, night robbed us of the chance to see the kill. I marvelled at his circling, his waiting, his secretiveness, his timing. It reminded me of a terrorist ambush.

The next morning on our drive I had illegally left our jeep to scout on foot. We saw two jeeps about a hundred yards away. There was a shout, then they turned and sped away from us. It seemed odd behaviour. Later I discovered that the drivers had mistaken us for terrorist intruders!

Late in the afternoon a large male leopard yawns, but concentrates on his prey.

Whenever the trackers saw a leopard, they shouted, "Kotiya!" I thought this interesting, because "kotiya" is actually the Sinhalese word for tiger. Leopard is correctly "diviya" for males and "dividena" for females. In fact, there are no tigers in Sri Lanka – except for the Tamil Tigers. I used to joke with Gillian, "I came to Sri Lanka to find leopards, but all I've found are Tigers."

In 1982 a leopard inhabited the rocks near the town of Amparai in the Gal Oya district. It was a bold one. First it attacked goats, then cattle, then the village dogs. One morning it was found in the maternity ward of Amparai's hospital. The villagers scared it away with flares and noises, but it kept returning. Finally wildlife authorities were called in, and they managed to trap the leopard by luring it into a cage baited with a dog and a monkey. The leopard went to the Colombo Zoo, and Amparai returned to normal.

After a breakfast of chick peas and strong coffee, we left Heenwewa shortly after four in the morning to meet Nihal Fernando, his wife, Dodo, and their daughter, Anu, at the Buttuwa bungalow. The sun came up over the Uraniya Plains as a huge red ball bursting through the morning clouds, silhouetting the buffalo, deer, and sambur beside a shallow lagoon.

We reached Buttuwa by ten. During our late breakfast Shirley Perera came by with more bad news. The Tigers had just captured Kumana and were encircling about two hundred Tamil National Army supporters on the beach at Pothana. Some fifty had escaped, however, and were reported fleeing in the direction of the Talgasmankada bungalow. He urged us to get out of there as soon as possible, so we went back, packed our gear, and returned to stay with the Fernandos in Buttuwa for two days.

Certainly the political situation was deteriorating. There seemed to be less and less the government could do to stop the conflict between its enemy's factions, particularly since India seemed intent on stoking the feud as a way of destabilizing Sri Lanka and bringing the island state under its own influence.

On the way to Tissa an old man told us of how he once saved one of his calves from a marauding leopard. Though he struck the leopard with a blow from a pole made of weera wood, the cat would not leave its prey.

Nihal Fernando's Land Rover was eighteen years old, but well equipped with shelves and perches for photography. He did his own driving, while Anu, Anver, and I stood in the back, eyes watchful and cameras ready. I noticed how Nihal was more interested in recording the beauty of what was before him than in capturing drama and action, both of which attracted me. As a result of that, or because I was less likely to get to Yala again, I found myself in more of a hurry. Nihal was happy to wait an hour for a special moment; I was too eager to snap and bash on. Despite our different techniques, however, we had a great time together.

The day before, Nihal told me, he had seen two leopards trying to carry a buffalo calf up into a tree, without success because of its weight. Today we saw a crocodile, more deer, and many birds at a water hole, but the only leopard sighting was of a female relaxing in the sand by the side of the track.

The rooming house that my mother ran in London became a financial success, and eventually she was hired by Sir Charles Forte to run the banqueting business at the Café Royale. This was a step up for her, and it meant a move to better living quarters, from the basement to a large, upstairs flat on Pembridge Crescent. More room meant more friends and guests, as people flocked to see my mother and often ended up staying the night.

My mother did more than tolerate this madness: she adored it. It kept her young and in the swim, and she seemed really happy. Although she often talked about my father and the old life, I never felt she missed it. Later on, as we grew more prosperous, she brought my brother, Michael, out from Ceylon to go to school in England and bought herself a house in Dulwich.

When Michael emigrated to Canada, Mother moved back to a flat in Chelsea, which had remained the centre of her social life. She was in her element. She entertained, took trips to Paris and North

In the early 1960s my mother moved back to Chelsea, which remained the centre of her social life in England.

America, saw her brother, Noel, frequently, and continued to live life at a hectic pace. Perhaps nothing has made me happier than to see her so happy in her last years, a life of freedom, fun, and friends.

I was playing tennis in Bermuda when I heard that she had died. It was a terrible shock, but oh, what an extraordinary funeral! The church in Chelsea was crowded, and people were standing on the street – busboys from the Criterion, chambermaids, ambassadors, bank employees, old guests, school friends, lords and ladies, all mingling companionably. No one could be sad. She had always told me that she didn't want a funeral, she wanted a party. She wanted the party to end all parties, and we gave her that.

The last person left her flat on the King's Road around two in the morning. It was Lady Corea's sister, Pearlie Saranavanamuttu. I had been telling her that the only time my mother had ever let me down was once when I asked her to smuggle an Ivan Pieris painting out of Colombo. She had done it, all right, but had forgotten the name of the ship's captain to whom she had entrusted it. I was upset, but nothing could make her remember the name. Pearlie couldn't believe her ears. Just the night before, someone had told her about a package that he was supposed to deliver in London, but he had lost the address. Apparently the package contained the painting. Now Pearlie dashed to the telephone, tracked down the courier, and asked him if my mother's name was the one he had misplaced. Yes, it was, and within forty minutes I had the wonderful painting *The Lovers* in my hands. It now hangs in the bedroom of my house in England.

I have never had a moment's doubt that all this had been organized by my mother as a last laugh from somewhere beyond the grave.

Edmund Wilson, Yala's current game warden, came to dinner, which was fun because he proved to be an excellent raconteur. The year before, for example, he had found a two-week-old elephant that had fallen into a well at Situlpahuwa. It managed to stay afloat by paddling for an entire night, until Edmund and eight villagers roped it out of the water. They fed it buffalo milk, put it in his jeep, and set off to find its herd. But whenever Edmund tried to leave it with the adult elephants, the baby elephant preferred to follow the jeep. Eventually the adult elephants themselves surrounded the jeep until the baby felt adopted by them. Then they cleared a way and let Edmund drive off – a wonderful example of co-operation between man and beast.

He also told some gruesome tales from the few years he had spent training in Tanzania. There, he said, the trainees were ordered to slaughter elephants, baboons, and hippopotami to clear the area for cultivation. The ivory, meat, and skins were either sold for revenue or given to the local tribes. Obviously a lot of the students didn't want to participate in the massacres, but they were warned they wouldn't graduate if they didn't.

His experience confirmed the impression I had received in Africa that the trade in ivory and skins was sanctioned secretly by high levels of government because of its value in hard currency and because of tribal politics. There was definitely some poaching in Sri Lanka, but I sensed that the people really loved and respected their wildlife, though the difference may have been due merely to Sri Lanka's relative abundance of land, water, and food.

The night at Buttuwa brought back a flood of memories, for here was where I had stayed with my father in 1946. The original bungalow, dating from 1938, was completely renovated in 1954 and again in 1962, so that it barely resembled the small primitive structure I remembered; but the sea in front, the rocks to the side, and the sound of the sea breaking on the rocks were vividly familiar. Before going to sleep fanned by the cool and scented breeze and lulled by the gentle crash of waves, I thought of how much had changed since my last visit. My father broken and then dead. The boy now a man. The peaceful and prosperous imperial colony become a war-torn and poor Third World nation. Lives coming and going with the waves. Empires rising and falling with the waves. Factions fighting and dying with the waves. Kingdoms, corporations, families, individuals up for a moment of glory and down into decay and ruin with the waves. Animals killing and being killed with the waves. Waves, waves, waves, waves.

By special permission, I was allowed to do the dune walk, a two-mile hike along the coast from Debaragaswala back to Buttuwa, with Anver the tracker. It is usually prohibited because of the danger of being out in the open, on foot, and without weapons. A jeep is a kind of zoo in reverse. You're in the cage, so the animals feel safe. When you're "on the loose," they feel vulnerable, and you become another predator to them.

We drove south before dawn and parked our jeeps by the road, then walked in the pitch dark through scrub until we came to the beach. This walk was short, no more than fifteen minutes, but I found myself feeling extremely nervous. Our arrival at the more open sandy expanse came as a relief. The shoreline was marked by the great dunes, twenty feet high or so, which had to be climbed like hills and descended like steep valleys. The sea was silvery and strangely silent at that hour, as the predawn light rose over its horizon. We were full of anticipation. Dawn and dusk are the times the animals love to venture out into this openness.

Villagers bathing baby elephants – a regular occurrence where there is a convenient river.

Within minutes we were stalking sambur in a sand hollow. As big and heavy as elk, they are the largest deer in Sri Lanka. The stags with their horns can make a wonderful photograph against the morning glow, but they are very wary and easily spooked. We got within twenty yards of them but there was still hardly enough light to shoot a picture.

We moved on. Our feet sank into the clear, fine sand that had been blown smooth by the soft winds. Our tracks joined other tracks, of small deer, of crabs, of wild boar, but none yet of elephants or leopards. I knew, however, that leopards preferred the security of the thickets that lined the beach. They emerged only to pounce on prey that came within reach. A hunter named Harry Storey described in his book *Hunting and Shooting in Ceylon* what happened to him when he encountered a leopard on a walk. He had stopped for a moment to rest when, suddenly, his old guide went running by in panic.

I gazed at him, uncomprehending, in surprise, when, glancing towards the forest, I saw a full-grown, but small and thickset, leopard emerge from the jungle like a flash. It passed me at about five yards, perfectly silent, going not in leaps and bounds but belly to the ground like a greyhound, and catching up to the old man, sprang on to his back, the impetus knocking the man down, so that they both rolled head over heels.

The leopard landed fair on the man's back and shoulders, its forepaws catching him round the neck, and its head, with its murderous jaws wide open, actually lay on top of the man's cap. The shock knocked the old man down, and he rolled head over heels, the leopard, being shot off him by the fall, also rolling head over heels beyond him. By this time, of course, I had my rifle ready, as I expected the brute, on rising, would go for the old man and thus give me a chance of a shot. However, it did nothing of the sort. It recovered its feet in an instant and launched itself at me, all in one movement, so to speak, without any pause, and with such fearful rapidity that, prepared as I was, I had only just time to throw my rifle to my shoulder and pull the trigger without seeing a sight or anything – a regular snapshot.

If I never saw "battle, murder, and sudden death" before, I saw it coming towards me then, in awful silence, mouth wide open, showing some very unpleasantly powerful teeth, ears laid back, and eyes fixed on me with a baneful glare; but at my shot the flying figure collapsed and came rolling over and over to my very feet. As quick as I thought I dropped my rifle, and pulling out my hunting-knife, a big heavy one with a double-edged blade, plunged it into the brute behind the shoulder.

Well and good if I had stabbed and withdrawn the knife very quickly; but I did not. Like an ass I wrenched it about in the wound a bit, with the result of galvanising the leopard into comparatively active life, for it turned suddenly over, knocked

Land monitor with early-morning kill.

120

the knife flying out of my hand, grabbed me by the left leg with its forepaws, and pulled me down on top of it. I rolled over to one side at once, kicked desperately at it with my right foot, whilst my left hand was occupied fending its horrible head away from my face, as we lay side by side, for it was struggling hard to get its teeth into me. Trying to set it by the throat, my left hand unfortunately got into its mouth, and it promptly took hold hot and strong. So I had to leave it at that, but thrust its head away to the full stretch of my arm and then got to work pulling its claws out of me.

This I succeeded in doing after a while, and by a desperate wrench getting my left hand free, rolled rapidly over; but I was not quick enough, for out came a paw, got me by the thigh, and hauled me back again. More kicking and struggling, and again I got free, but again the awful paw hauled me back like a bundle of old clothes. Another desperate effort and I managed to roll out of reach, got up, staggered to my rifle, reloaded and shot the brute dead; and then, as the whole universe seemed to be going round and round in a variety of colours, I dropped to the ground to consider matters a bit, feeling deathly sick. However, it was getting late, so I soon arose and began to inspect the damage. I perceived my left trousers leg to be dyed brilliant scarlet, as was my shoe, and, on pulling up the trousers, two of the various tears and holes in my leg spouted blood out about a foot, which sight fairly startled me. I yelled to the old man to get me a stick, but he seemed too dazed, so I twisted my handkerchief round my leg as tight as I could without the help of a stick, and then got up to have a look at the man. He was torn a bit down the back, round the neck, and one claw had penetrated very close to the throat. I wrapped one of his cloths round his neck to stop the streaming blood, and we turned towards camp, a terrible two miles away. My wounds got very painful and stiff, and my left hand was about useless; but we struggled on, getting to camp whilst there was still light enough to see our way.

Towards the end of our dune walk, after about two hours, we heard the bark of a spotted deer and the anguished call of a young buffalo. A leopard kill, I thought. Instead of fear, I felt exhilaration: a chance to get a rare photograph of leopards feeding! "Let's go in," I said.

The commotion had come from far up one of the estuaries that coursed out of the jungle. Anver led me through the thorn thickets towards gruff, purring sounds. Two leopards, he signalled.

We crouched and crawled slowly on our hands and knees under the thorns, which pricked our backs and necks each time we needed to straighten up. After ten minutes we came to a small clearing just to the left of the estuary. Anver was lying on his stomach immediately ahead of me. I touched his ankle, and when he turned around, he saw a leopard looking in at us at the edge of the water. We both saw it, and we both saw it being joined by a second leopard. They were perhaps thirty yards away. Clearly agitated, they continued to stare at us, eyeball to eyeball, but nobody moved.

After a minute we realized they weren't going to attack. It was just as well, because our only defence would have been the knobbed stick that Anver was holding in his right hand. I took a couple of photographs, but the light was poor and the shots almost certainly out of focus.

"Let's go round to their other side," I whispered to Anver. "I need the sun behind me when it comes up."

We turned carefully, with me now leading, and retraced our path back to the beach. Then we walked directly up the estuary, backs straight. Rounding a corner we came directly into the path of one of the leopards!

It wasn't more than twenty yards away and, worse, it was as surprised as we were. It turned and crouched as if to spring and, in that moment, I instinctively raised my camera and banged two quick shots. The leopard seemed to change its mind. It turned again and headed rapidly into the jungle.

We never saw the leopard again, nor any signs of a kill, but I had had my exhausting and thrilling rush and had stalked a leopard on foot. I knew I should have been scared, but instead I discovered the remarkable sense of security that takes over when you face danger while looking through the lens of a camera.

Back at the bungalow for breakfast Nihal told us that his most perilous moment had also been on the dunes.

During his last visit he had come across a solitary elephant, and by misfortune he had stepped between it and the jungle. It must have felt trapped, because it charged him. Elephants can run fast, and Nihal had trouble running in the deep sand, so it was a near thing. Oddly enough, the elephant waited for Nihal to return along the dunes, then chased him again.

"Clashes continue," said the small headline; "455 killed in 30 days," blared another.

I never worried as much about the wild animals as I did about the armed terrorists and the trigger-happy soldiers. On days driving around Yala when we seemed to be the only people around I still often had the ominous feeling that we weren't alone. Several times I was sure we were being watched by hidden eyes in the jungle.

Nihal managed to shift my focus for an afternoon from leopards to trees, although I kept hoping to see leopards in the trees: the palu, the weera, the kumbuk, the wood apple, the halmilla, the malitthan (the biblical mustard tree), the thelembu (the oil of whose black seeds is used to lubricate cart wheels). We watched the different greens create a splendid kaleidoscope of patterns that changed with the varying light, from yellow morning to white noon, to tangerine evening. As the huge sun slipped gently but quickly below the horizon, leaving the trees silhouetted against the glow, the shriek of the peacocks was joined by a chorus of terns, lapwings, ibises, egrets, pond herons, and sandpipers. Nothing else disturbed the tranquillity.

In fact, the Buttuwa bungalow seemed so still that it never felt part of the jungle. The sea had replaced the animal and bird noises at night. An old cow elephant lingered around, there was the occasional mongoose or snake, a pair of sea eagles hovered over the shore, but there wasn't the ruckus of monkeys and deer and birds I had become used to. The peace, the pleasure, and the long days made sleep delightfully easy.

Yet when the sun rose, all the animals and birds came to life as if on cue. One morning I saw a strange thing. A herd of spotted deer was ambling along the shore. When the dawn changed from silver to gold, they burst into a run and the two larger stags reared up on their hind legs, thrusting their long antlers into the glorious sky.

Nihal's daughter, Anu, told me about Bandara, the best tracker in the Wilpattu National Park and a great friend of her family. He had the ability to spot a leopard in the twisted configurations of shaded branches by the mere twitch of the cat's ear, and he could tell from one glance at a paw mark in the sand how much time had elapsed since the leopard had passed.

In May 1985, according to most reports, the Tamil Tigers launched one of the bloodiest massacres in Sri Lankan history. Terrorists stormed into the ancient city of Anuradhapura and mowed down one hundred and twenty-eight Buddhist pilgrims, some of whom were worshipping at the sacred Bo tree. The killers then escaped through the Wilpattu park en route to the west coast. At the entrance they slaughtered twenty-three members of the staff. Then they took Bandara to show them the way through the jungle. They were making for Pookulam, thirty-six miles away, where boats were waiting to carry them off. They shot Bandara dead before they embarked. He was forty-two years old.

Childers Jayawardhana and Nihal Fernando on the dunes near Buttuwa.

At eleven o'clock we moved again, to the bungalow at Patanangala. It was only a few miles from Buttuwa, but newer and right on the beach. Instead of the breakers smashing on the rocks, small waves lapped the sand, and instead of the harsh glare around Buttuwa the ingini trees cast a wonderful shade. The strong easterly wind kept us cooler too, so that we noticed the contrast immediately whenever we drove away from it into Yala's interior. It was a comfortable place, except for the flies, which were a major nuisance. Nothing worked to keep them off.

The flies probably were attracted by the nearby fishing camp. Each season nomadic fishermen come and build on the beach a temporary village of thatched huts, which they burn when they leave for their homes in Tangalla or Kudawella. Mostly migrant Sinhalese, they have coarse and weather-beaten features and seem quite different in manner from the other Sinhalese and Tamils. I used to see them set out for the morning catch at four o'clock. Every day we would pick up a seer, jack, mullet, or barracuda for the cook at the bungalow, but the local supply of fish was limited. Most of it is sold at a guaranteed price to a company that is half owned by the government.

At the edge of the village of Patanangala there is an extraordinary outcropping of rock. It lifts out of the sea to some four hundred feet, absolutely smooth and rounded. Villagers often climb it for the spectacular view of the ocean and the coastal lighthouse that is the last landmark before the South Pole. I also saw sloth bears walking over it, dark and shaggy creatures that have to be approached with care. They have little fondness for or fear of people, and are said to have killed more humans in Sri Lanka than the leopards have.

There is a lot of water in the jungle surrounding the rock, so there is a lot of wildlife, especially elephants. As these elephants had been known to charge villagers, we were warned not to venture out alone. We were warned also not to swim out too far in the sea, because its tides and currents were severe enough to sweep you away. And we were again warned about terrorists. They were in the area and sometimes hid in the outcropping.

Edmund Wilson came for dinner and brought disturbing news. M.M.D. Perera, the assistant director of the wildlife department's eastern region, and three other officials had been murdered. The perpetrators were reported to be members of the Tamil National Army. The attack on the victims' jeep had

A grey langur monkey high on a branch in the bright morning light.
Overleaf: A fishing village in Patanangala. The extraordinary outcropping of rock in the background rises some four hundred feet above the sea.

happened less than thirty miles from where we were staying.

Among the dead was a gamekeeper named Arulanandan. His murder was a profound shock to us. "Arul" had been a close friend of Childers and Nihal Fernando, and they had arranged for me to meet him when I went north to Polonnaruwa. In fact, his reputation as a tracker was so strong that we had planned to take our final trip with him from Polonnaruwa. Anu, Nihal's daughter, told me all about him and later wrote an appreciation of Arul that appeared in a Colombo newspaper. I felt I had met the old man with the big bushy moustache when I read it:

He was a big man, tall and robust, with a deep, humorous voice and an endless repertoire of stories. Whenever we visited Kumana he was our companion and he led us here, there, everywhere, talking all the time. He introduced me to that desolate bay of Kirigalla where time stands still, Bovattagala where rocks and caverns tumble in glorious array, Bambaragastalawa and its Buddha statue, the precincts of which are never desecrated by a falling leaf, the cave of Kiripokunahela and its vedda drawing of a leopard leaping onto a man riding an elephant. He rowed us into Kumana villu where thousands of storks nested in noisy mêlée. Once the boat capsized, Arul emerged from beneath the murky waters festooned in algae and small crabs, laughing and laughing. We sat under a Dun tree at Thunmulla and watched a herd of buffalo swim across the villu. When I got up to leave, "Wait," said he. So I waited and watched as a male buffalo bounded past us to plunge into the villu and disappear into the jungle in the tracks of the retreating herd. Soon he returned having rounded up his harem, which had temporarily adopted another leader, and the whole herd swam once more across the glinting waters as the sun set on the horizon.

Arul knew, loved and respected his animals. His special skill lay with the bull elephants of Kumana. They were unpredictable and cantankerous. When returning after a long day in the jungle we were confronted by a huge elephant who stood in the centre of the road and calmly surveyed us. The party ahead of us turned round to take the longer route home. Not so with Arul. He alighted from the Rover, sat on the bonnet and started talking to the elephant. "No room on the road for the two of us," said he. "We are not turning. You would have to." The elephant listened, flapping its ears. Gradually Arul's voice rose and finally he began to yell. The elephant tolerated this treatment for about fifteen minutes and then he went away walking backwards, his eyes never leaving Arul.

While sitting on the banks of the Kumbukkan Oya I recall Arul quietly laying a hand on my knee and whispering, "Do not move." I froze while a snake slithered over his foot and my foot and crawled into the overgrowth. At Divulpallama, we found a buffalo half-buried in the mud. Its struggles to rise were in vain because its legs were in the air and it could not get a firm foothold. The buffalo of Kumana are dangerous animals and they have gored many people. Arul went up to the buffalo, caught its rear legs and with a superhuman heave swung them around and ran for cover while the buffalo thundered into the jungle. I remember him watching as the children of an important government official ran about gathering mementoes. "Drop those," said he and he sat down beside them on a rock and spoke to them of the sanctity of the forest, of environment and ecology, of the destructive collector's instinct, of ashes to ashes, dust to dust. And then he gave them each a small fragment of bone which they accepted in awe with gentle hand.

When I met him last year in Kumana Arul was a sad man. His country was dying. The vast grasslands where deer and buffalo roamed were deserted. The Bagura plains were a charred dust-bowl. The department staff quarters and the Thunmulla bungalow were razed to the ground. Okanda bungalow was a skeleton. Law and order had broken down completely. He spoke of the countless number of people that walked into Kumana for a countless number of reasons. Truckloads of deer were being shot and removed. Even the eggs of nesting birds had become targets. More dangerous forces threatened his domain.

Those dangerous forces ultimately killed him. The son of Tamils and married to a Tamil, he was rumoured to be a Tiger sympathizer. Clearly, whatever his political sympathies, he was a marked man in the eyes of the Tamil National Army. I too might have been a marked man had I met him and gone travelling with him as planned.

Shirley Perera (no relation to M.M.D. Perera) had had his own encounter with terrorists. Two years earlier he had been captured and imprisoned by the Tamil Tigers, and his prison became the centre of a battle between the Tigers and the Sri Lankan army. A sane and cool-headed man, Shirley hid in a lavatory until the shooting stopped and the Tigers fled. Then he came out with his hands over his head, yelling, "Wildlife! Wildlife!" He was one of the lucky few to survive such a capture. Later he would laugh off the incident as part of his job.

A slow day on the plains, hot and very dusty, with few animals and fewer visitors. We disturbed a red-wattled lapwing on her nest, which was well camouflaged among dried buffalo dung on the burnt grass. Her three spotted eggs seemed far too large for a small water bird.

At noon, returning to the bungalow, we were stopped by a staff vehicle and told that the Sri Lankan army had moved into Yala to halt the advance of the Tamil National Army across the park. The murder of M.M.D. Perera and his staff had alerted the government to the seriousness of the situation, which would become even more serious if the park fell under the control of either Tamil faction. I realized that the Sri Lankan army was in a difficult position. It had to maintain order without siding – or appearing to side – with either the TNA or the Tamil Tigers.

Yala seemed suspiciously silent and deserted all afternoon. We were alone on our drive, but with no clue as to why. Since neither Childers nor Lucky knew any more than I about what was going on, I insisted we speed the eight miles to the park's headquarters for information. My guess was that the park had been closed, and it seemed a good guess when we saw an army jeep with six soldiers in battle dress near the entrance. They ordered us not to take any pictures of them, as if shy of publicity. But Edmund Wilson said the publicity was already out. The park wasn't officially closed; people were just afraid to come. He wasn't sure how much protection the army could offer, nor how close the TNA was, but he didn't think we were immediately threatened.

Both Childers and Lucky seemed more subdued than usual, and from the little Sinhalese I understood, I knew they were thinking about leaving the park earlier than planned. I convinced them to stay on, however. We were confident that Edmund Wilson or Shirley Perera would advise us if the situation worsened, and we rather liked the idea of having the park to ourselves.

Before dinner the keeper at the Yala bungalow and his assistant showed up for the night. They had heard that officials bringing the staff pay had been attacked and killed, and they felt safer at Patanangala. Like the other park staff, they looked nervous. The rumours and the lack of hard facts were even more upsetting than the confirmed bad news. Nor was the presence of the Sri Lankan army much comfort. It was made up largely of thousands of young men, some mere boys of eighteen. Certainly few were used to jungle combat in unfamiliar territory, so they often were as skittish as the wild animals.

On my last day in Yala I wanted to go back to the rock where we had seen the mating leopards. But it was as strangely lifeless as the rest of the park. The day was overcast, cooler and gloomier.

We held a farewell feast of fish curry for Shirley Perera. He reported that the TNA soldiers had scattered farther into the jungle, the Tamil Tigers were in firm control of Kumana, and the Sri Lankan army was stationed nearby.

He also remembered another incident involving a man-eating leopard. In 1972 he was sent to investigate the death of a man who had been on a pilgrimage to the holy shrine on top of Adam's Peak. It was clear to Shirley that the pilgrim had been killed by a leopard, but in the absence of any witness the official record stated only that his body had been partially eaten by a leopard. The nearby villagers confirmed Shirley's judgement that leopards kill humans much more often than the authorities admit.

The leopards must have been as lazy as I felt that afternoon. Either they had had as big a lunch as I had, or they were wiser than I about leaving their shaded resting place, for I saw only birds: three varieties of bee-eaters, two varieties of herons, as well as egrets, bush larks, hornbills, tank eagles, sunbirds, and a red-backed woodpecker.

That didn't prevent me from getting into trouble, however. I was photographing a pair of Parson's storks, using the mudguard of Nihal Fernando's jeep as a tripod, when he started yelling in a sharp and agitated fashion, "Pelican, Christopher, there's a pelican!" Or at least that's what I thought he was saying. In fact, there was an elephant, an enormous male just coming into musth, heading directly my way at about ten feet. I got to my jeep as the elephant trampled over the spot where I had been standing. A close call!

During one of the many philosophical discussions Lucky and I had during the days we passed together, I asked him why he didn't work harder and apply his intelligence to business.

"Why should I?" he answered. "What's the point of sweating for money? I might be killed at any time."

He wasn't looking for danger, he wasn't even bothered greatly by danger, but he was always aware of danger. It took from him that drive that pushes North Americans, but it gave to him a *laissez-faire* approach to life that we might envy.

The first part of my trip was over. I had gleaned lots of information about leopards, their relationship to people, and their dominant position on the island. With this research behind me I felt better prepared for my journey to Punanai.

Reports of disturbances had been following us around Yala, and now they followed us out. Having packed the night before, we were away in pitch darkness and in Tissa by dawn. There we saw a newspaper with the headline,

"Lawyer hacked to death at Embilipitiya." It had caught my eye because we were heading for Embilipitiya to have breakfast with Childers's aunt and uncle, whose home was on the way to my next goal, the Kuttapitiya tea estate on which I had grown up. I was curious to ask them what they knew about this latest killing.

They proved to be a quaint old couple living in a colonial house full of Sri Lankan relics and antiques. So I was shocked when they explained in a casual way that the lawyer had "had it coming to him," because he had been engaged in devious political activities.

I was back among mankind, its laws and its savagery, and I was already starting to miss the open spaces, the silent hours, and the natural ways of birds and beasts.

An enormous male elephant just coming into musth trampled over the spot where I had been standing only a few seconds earlier. A close call!

4

Interval

It is eighty miles from Tissamaharama to Pelmadulla, but it had taken me forty-three years to get back to the town where I had spent the greater part of my early years. Pelmadulla had grown, of course, in population and busyness, to the degree that I had trouble finding my way around it. There were even small villages surrounding it. I had a photograph taken of myself standing under the sign at the entrance to the Kuttapitiya Tea and Rubber Estate.

Kuttapitiya had been one of the most prosperous estates in Ceylon, though generally less prosperous than those at higher elevations in the cooler climate. In my father's time it was managed by Carson's, and all its four thousand acres were under cultivation. Now it was a division of a nationalized undertaking, with only one thousand acres in operation. The deterioration was evident immediately in the four miles of steeply winding road up to the bungalow. The road was much worse and in places barely passable. We took almost forty minutes to reach the top. I remembered the hairpin curves. Many of them you couldn't take in a single sweep unless you were brave and swung out to the edge of the precipice before making a sharp turn to the left or right. Our driver usually had to stop and back up to get around the corners, but my father used to be bolder because he knew the road better and had a natural bravado. He often passed within six inches of the edge in a frighteningly erratic swing, but as far as I knew he made a bad mistake only that one time with my sisters and me after he had been drinking.

As we wound our way up, I savoured the familiar view. High banks of tea

Workers gathering dried manna grass for thatching roofs.
Previous page: High banks of tea bushes cover the great slopes above, beside, and below the road up to Kuttapitiya, once my father's estate.

bushes covered the great slopes above, alongside, and below us with a luxurious green. The bushes were thick and about three feet high, and every dozen yards they were interrupted by the glidicidia trees that lent them a crucial shade. Between the rows moved the Tamil women workers, who plucked the shoots and threw them in the baskets they bore on their backs, then carried the baskets to the factory for weighing, drying, processing, packaging, and shipping. As we neared the factory, I could smell the strong and pungent aroma of tea, and I found myself reciting the five grades: "Broken orange pekoe, orange pekoe, pekoe, fannings, and dust."

The labourers had been brought by the British from India, so their history and culture differed from those of the Tamils who had migrated to northern Ceylon centuries before. As a boy I had been horrified by the discomfort of their living quarters. They lived in what were called "coolie lines," long rooms under a tin roof, with primitive latrines. Now, I was told, conditions were better; certainly I saw more huts along the road.

The bungalow had been built by a planter who had cut off the peak of the hill and put a lovely house in the middle of a garden with a view of the Pelmadulla valley – or sometimes just of an ocean of clouds. An unpretentious one-storey structure, it was beautiful in its simplicity and openness. I was delighted to find that it had been kept up by the current manager, Alistair Perera, who was kind enough to let me wander around his home alone with my memories.

I recognized the maroon red of the concrete floor, the rattan furniture, the old Dutch chairs with the cane seats, my room, the nursery, my father's old

Kuttapitiya, now a division of the Sri Lanka State Plantations Corporation, had been one of the most prosperous estates in Ceylon.

office, my parents' bedroom, the servants' quarters, the lawn where I had dug a pit to practise high-jumping. In what had been my father's office I saw the old black phone that held the direct lines to the tea factory and to the general office. In the dining-room I found above his chair the two holes in the wall from which had hung the large Lionel Wendt drawing of a nude. Though much was missing, I felt I had walked into my yesterdays. I could hear my father ringing the brass bell with a hit of his hand to summon a servant to fetch his gin or his burnt toast. I could see my father getting up abruptly from his chair, causing Tuppence, the cocker spaniel, and Chindit, the spaniel-beagle, to scurry away, their paws skidding on the polished floor. I could imagine my mother at work in her beloved rock garden. It was still there and still blooming.

We had moved into this idyllic bungalow from another on the estate when my father was promoted to manager. I was nine. It seemed a paradise, a garden above the clouds, a private idyll cut off from the rest of the world. The awful roads and the long distances between the estates meant that we were usually self-contained as a family, except when visitors came or we were sent to school. It was an outdoor existence, and I spent the days playing with my sisters, walking with my father, going into the jungle with the locals. It was also an English existence, with servants and dinner parties and Western food. (I loved curry but got it only when I begged for it.) Sometimes we would go down to the tennis club in Pelmadulla for games or dances, but generally we were alone, and happy to be alone. I hated having to go away to school at the age of six, first to St. Thomas's in Colombo, then up country to Gurutalawalla, then to Ootacamund in southern India, and I craved my return to the estate.

Though my father could be kind and lenient to a fault, he could also be a tyrant. He was happiest doing the simplest things: being with his family, running the estate, discussing the book he was reading, teaching his children, talking to people.

Oddly enough, the bungalow had a reputation as an unlucky place. (I still get eerie vibrations whenever I walk into a house that seems ominous or doomed.) My mother actually begged my father not to take the senior job because of the accidents, deaths, or other misfortunes that had struck former residents.

I do not believe that the place destroyed my father, but his destruction always seemed a mystery to me. We were so happy that I couldn't understand why he wasn't happy and why he had to drink. He had brains and charisma, he was an avid reader and a keen naturalist, he adored his family and liked people, but he seemed very frustrated and full of self-contempt. Perhaps the dark side came from the shadow of my grandfather, whose drive, legal aptitude, and financial success made him a powerful and intimidating model. My father may have been a better planter and had better rapport with others, but he lacked his father's stamina for work and hunger for achievement. Law and finance interested him less than drama and literature, yet he felt compelled to try his hand at wealth and success. His failure irked him and may have killed him.

Though he could be kind and lenient to a fault, he could also be a tyrant. Though he could be very loving, he always expected things to be done his way. And though he could be vulnerable, he sometimes reduced everything to rubble with his thoughtlessness, his drunkenness, his borrowing, and his irresponsibility towards his business and, sometimes, his family. At root, I suspect that, despite his very attractive qualities and his aristocratic demeanour, he lacked self-esteem. This lack perhaps stemmed from the awe in which he held my grandfather, and also perhaps from being the only Ceylonese among Carson's Scottish and English tea agents. Despite his initial competence as a manager, he never felt he fulfilled the expectations of either, and when the appearance of moderate success collapsed, he had no inner confidence to fall back on.

Mervyn Ondaatje was happiest doing the simplest things: being with his family, running the estate, discussing the books he was reading, teaching his children, talking to people. Somehow he thought he had to aim higher in order to be happy. He didn't have to. He shouldn't have tried to. But "the devil drives," and it drove him to his sad end. And his sad end drove me because of my own frustration and loss.

Then I knew that it was not just lack of time and pressure of work that had prevented my return to this place for more than forty years. Shame had kept me away too. Because I was ashamed of what had happened to my father and our family, I never wanted to return as a nobody. Now I was considered a somebody. I could have filled my days in Sri Lanka with appointments to see top politicians, VIPs, and diplomats. That knowledge gave me some pride, but it wasn't what had brought me here, to the estate. I had come back to Kuttapitiya to try to recover what I had lost.

Standing again in our home I felt the full impact of that loss. I missed my childhood. I missed my mother and father. I had achieved more than they ever dreamed of, because I had my grandfather's drive and dedication, but I couldn't replace what they and I had loved most. My father broke his family, and now it was just pieces of memory, some old furniture and a view, two holes

As we came down the terrible Kuttapitiya estate road people came out of nowhere to greet me, shaking my hand and calling me "Ondaatje Putha."

in a wall, an old black phone, a brass bell, and a garden of rocks.

I had to hold back my tears when, after two hours, we descended the steep, rough, winding road back down to the Pelmadulla valley. Would I ever come again? Would I ever have to? The road had deteriorated so badly that I was afraid the car would be damaged, and in places I got out and walked to make sure we missed the holes and rocks. And as we descended, people appeared out of nowhere to greet me, shaking my hand and calling me, "Ondaatje Putha," Ondaatje son.

Near the bottom of the road I saw a dozen people standing beside their simple homes. One of them shouted, "Good afternoon," in English. He was a very elderly man who then asked if I recognized him. He had been my mother's carpenter. I recalled my mother having furniture made, but I couldn't place him until he asked if I remembered the school boxes he had made for me. And then he came back to me, as a young man with thick black hair. Immediately he began to mimic my mother's voice, yelling, "Come, come, children. Come, come, come. Hurry up. Hurry up. Daddy's waiting." Not only was it her tone, but he even imitated the haughty angle of her chin. Everyone laughed at the memory, and for a moment I was back in my wild and carefree childhood.

As we drove towards Colombo through the verdant rice fields of the Ratnapura valley, we passed the gem pits, damp and muddy shafts propped up with wooden beams, from which are scooped rubies, amethysts, emeralds, sapphires, and other precious or semi-precious stones. When I was young and out driving with my father, he used to stop and buy rubies or sapphires as presents for my mother. Out of my sorrow came that tiny, shining image - his happiness, her happiness, my happiness at their happiness - as if it were a gem I had washed from a basketful of gravel pulled from the dark, muddy, and dangerous pit of the past.

That night, I had just come full circle, arriving back at Gillian's in Colombo, when the heat and humidity were broken by a tremendous tropical storm. The downpour came fast and furious, so fast that the courtyard filled with four inches of water, so furious that we had difficulty hearing each other speak at dinner. It seemed refreshing, however, after two weeks of arid wilderness. Appropriate, too, as if it were washing away the dust and dangers of Yala and joining the flood of memories and tears at Kuttapitiya.

The journey to Colombo took us past the Ratnapura gem pits – damp and muddy shafts propped up with wooden beams, from which are scooped rubies, amethysts, emeralds, sapphires, and other stones.

5
Punanai

The break was a brief one. After just a day spent gathering more supplies, we headed north on the second circuit towards Punanai.

The evening before our departure I had dinner with Gillian's daughter, Shaan, and her friend Sheahan. We talked mostly about photography. Sheahan understood, for example, about the false sense of security a camera gives – war photographers have often experienced it – and he told me of one incident when he was shooting the underside of an elephant's trunk and the inside of its mouth with a telescopic lens without realizing that the trunk was actually poised close enough to strike him on the head. He had been saved from serious injury only by the quick action of his driver.

Sheahan also cautioned me about my expedition north. The JVP rebels were now a real danger near Kandy and Sigiriya; the Tamil Tigers and the Tamil National Army were much in evidence near Anuradhapura and Polonnaruwa; and Punanai was out of the question. It was north of the so-called Tamil border, beyond the bounds of several army checkpoints, and in the midst of the conflict. "Madness," he concluded. When I made it clear I wasn't going to be discouraged, he said, "Well, try never to be alone, and try not to make yourself conspicuous."

A fisherman casting his net at dawn from an outrigger canoe.
Previous page: At noon on May 22, 1924, Captain R. Shelton Agar received a telegram from the Government Agent, Eastern Province, Ceylon. "Reward Rs. 100/ - offered destruction man-eating leopard Punanai ten miles from Valachenai ferry."

Vellupillai Prabakaran, the short, bearded, and enigmatic leader of the Tamil Tigers, is known to have a love for Clint Eastwood movies and leopards. Apparently he keeps two leopard cubs and is often photographed with them. They say he has studied the characteristics of the cats and likes to identify himself with them.

Childers and I left Colombo early and in style – that is, in an air-conditioned Honda car driven by Raja. Lucky was going to join us later with his jeep, once it had been serviced. Our first stop would be Rock Hill, my grandfather's old coconut plantation near Kegalle, fifty miles away.

There wasn't much comfort in what I saw, however. Since my father's death the estate's twenty-eight productive acres had been sold off into sixty-eight parcels of land, so that the country retreat now looked more like a fully populated village. We had to tread our way up narrow and rugged tracks to get to the old house, which looked a great deal older and smaller than I remembered. For years, I was told, it had been left unattended, a prey to looters, until it was bought as a rooming house by a certain Mr. Bandala. We met this gentleman, but he was less than hospitable, mistaking us for government inspectors or tax collectors. He probably had good reason to be afraid, because the house looked completely run-down. Eventually he opened the place and let me wander the rooms, conjuring up the ghosts of Christmases past when all the family used to gather here.

It had been a grander and more formal place than Kuttapitiya. When we went there, it was as if we were wild creatures who had to be cleaned up and dressed up for our special visits to my grandfather's. It wasn't as free or as much fun as at home; there wasn't the space in which to roam or run. Even so, Rock Hill meant holidays and cousins and the large HMV gramophone in Grandfather's library. I saw the rooms of my father and his sisters,

Our driver, Mahinda "Raja" Rajapakse. He was tireless and fearless and I could always rely on his judgement.

150

I saw the mangosteen tree in which we hid as children, and I saw the place where my father – shouting at his second wife in a drunken rage – had tripped on some matting at the entrance to the living-room off the veranda and smashed his head on the concrete floor.

People come and people go, just like at the Grand Hotel. Dynasties, economies, empires come and go in cycles long or short. Like my grandfather I have built my own house. However much I might wish it preserved, I won't be able to protect it after I die. My son will build his own house, my grandchildren may seek their fortunes in foreign lands, and villages and rooming houses may spring up where I have been happiest.

According to the *Mahavamsa*, Sri Lanka's equivalent of Homer's *Odyssey*, a prince was sent away by his father for misbehaviour. Fate carried Vijaya and his seven hundred men from India to Ceylon, supposedly in 483 B.C., the year of the Buddha's death. There he founded his own kingdom after conquering a local tribe, the Yakkas or Demon Tribe, and their terrible queen, Kuveni. Kuveni's children by Vijaya became Ceylon's ancient peoples, the Veddas.

Vijaya was also the founder of the Sinhalese people. He married an Indian princess, and though he died without a royal heir, his nephew Panduvasdeva was appointed to succeed him. The nephew's offspring became "the lion race" ("sinha" means lion), because Vijaya was supposed to be the grandson of a lion. In the legend his grandmother, a rebellious princess, ran off with a caravan that was subsequently attacked by a lion. "When the lion had taken his prey and was leaving the spot," it is written, "he beheld her from afar, and love laid hold on him, and he came towards her with waving tail and ears laid back." Their union produced a boy and a girl, but not lasting happiness. There was a violent argument, at the end of which the lion was killed by his son, Sinhabahu.

"And he went to the opening of the cave, and as soon as he saw the lion who came forward in love toward his son, he shot an arrow at him," the *Mahavamsa* reports. "The arrow struck the lion's forehead, but because of the tenderness toward his son it rebounded, and fell on the earth at the youth's feet. And so it fell out three times; then did the king of beasts grow wrathful, and the arrow sent at him struck him and pierced his body."

Overleaf: Adam's Peak. All four major religions in Sri Lanka – Buddhism, Hinduism, Islam, and Christianity – claim the 7,360-foot mountain as a holy place.

Sinhabahu became King of Lala and father of Vijaya, whom he exiled. It seems to be the pattern of Sinhalese kings to be wayward and aggressive youths who grow into serene and wise rulers. Where were my own serenity and wisdom, I often wondered, or those of my father? We, the son and grandson of a lion. We, the wayward and aggressive youths.

Up, up, up to Dickoya, the heart of the up-country tea estates. It was a luxuriant green land, with well-kept buildings and subtropical gardens. Tea pluckers dotted the slopes or carried their baskets along the roadside. We stopped often to photograph the Tamil women, their dark and slender bodies, their thin and chiselled faces with a red dot on their foreheads and gold studs in their noses. Invariably they flashed toothy smiles, either dazzling white or stained with betel juice. According to his own account, when the poet Pablo Neruda was Chile's consul in Colombo in 1929, he became so smitten by the beauty of the Tamil woman who cleaned his toilet each day that he was driven to rape her.

As soon as we checked into the Dickoya bungalow I rushed off again, to see the pickers winding their way in single file down the slopes in the evening light. Because the industry seemed so healthy and organized, I felt closer to my childhood home here than at Kuttapitiya, with its weeds and squatters and turpentine trees. I felt closer to my father here.

To the southeast stood Adam's Peak, mostly covered by cloud. Just before dusk, however, as if by a miracle, the sun pierced through the covering for a few moments, sending shafts of light streaking from behind the sacred peak, which became a lighthouse sending rays of colour across the world.

All four major religions in Sri Lanka claim the 7,360-foot mountain as a holy place. The Buddhists call it Sri Pada, the Sacred Footprint, because Gautama the Buddha is said to have left the imprint of his foot on the granite top of the mountain on one of his visits to the island. The Hindus call it Shivan Adipatham, the Creative Dance of Shiva. The Muslims insist it is where Adam first touched the earth when he was driven out of paradise. And many Christians claim that the footprint marked in a boulder at the summit is that of St. Thomas the apostle, who had preached in southern India. The mountain has been a destination for pilgrims since the eleventh century, and even I climbed to its shrine as a boy. My father, our driver, and I set off at midnight to begin the long and steep climb. We got there just before dawn. It was cold and the wind was howling around the small white structure that protects the print. The shrine was packed with pilgrims. As the light came up in the east, we all

Up-country Tamil tea pluckers on a luxuriant green slope.

looked west to catch sight of the magical triangle created as the dawn light cast the mountain's shadow upon the clouds below us. This configuration existed only for a moment; then the shadow seemed to come towards us quickly and engulf us with its blessing.

I didn't climb the mountain this time, but shortly before dawn I was wakened by Raja yelling, "Come quickly! Come quickly!" From the garden of the Dickoya bungalow Adam's Peak was a golden glow lit by the sun's rays against a black sky. Without the morning mists or the haze of day it stood out clearly. I could even see the steps going up to the shrine and the shrine itself. As the sun rose, the golden triangle faded into the landscape of ranges and the light of a fresh morning.

We retraced part of our way down the winding highway from Dickoya in order to rejoin the main road between Colombo and Kandy, eighty miles farther on. Kandy is the traditional centre of Sri Lankan culture, the old bastion of the Kandyan kingdom until it fell to the British in 1815, and the town where I was born in 1933. Set in a beautiful valley halfway between the coast and the highest settlements, it enjoys a particularly pleasant climate of warm days and cool nights; and though as congested as any Asian town, it has a slower and better-organized atmosphere, conditioned perhaps by the large lake, the Dalada Maligawa or Temple of the Tooth, the European ambience, and the imperial ruins in the centre of the small city.

Its atmosphere seemed even more tranquil from Castle Hill, the delightful colonial house where we were staying. Its comfort seemed a luxury after the bungalows of Yala. A cool breeze wafted over the veranda, from which we had a charming view of the town and lake below. It was not unlike the grand house nearby that had been owned by my ancestors. It's now a tourist showcase for Kandyan dances.

Though neither my father nor grandfather ever lived in Kandy, I always associated the family with it. We used to visit it regularly, and I used to hear about ancestors or cousins who were prominent Kandyans. One of them, for example, had been involved in the construction of the famous Peradeniya Gardens in the early nineteenth century, perhaps the best natural park in the world and even greater now than then because the trees have reached full maturity. And then there was the infamous legend of the time my father became the only person in history to stop the Kandy Perahera.

In this magnificent annual pageant, the Sacred Tooth Relic of the Buddha is

Worker sweeping grain to dry in the hot afternoon sun.

156

honoured in order to propitiate the guardian gods of Sri Lanka and bring prosperity and blessings on the nation. The procession is led by a majestic elephant carrying a casket containing a replica of the sacred tooth of the Buddha. A hundred splendidly caparisoned elephants, chieftains in glittering traditional costumes, musicians, drums, dancers, and acrobats accompany the relic on its stately journey from the temple by the lake, around the city and, finally, back to the temple, where it is enshrined once again.

According to the aforementioned infamous legend, one year during the festival my father was staying in the Queen's Hotel just across the lake from the temple, and in a crazed state after an alcoholic argument with my mother he walked to the route of the Perahera and threw himself on the ground immediately in front of the principal elephant!

I passed the afternoon going into antique shops looking for knives. Because of Kandy's history as the splendid court of civilized kings, it remains known for its music and dance and for the fine craftsmanship of its gold jewellery and carved daggers. The daggers are intricate and exquisite objects, with ivory handles inlaid with gems and blades struck from silver and gold.

In the evening we paid a brief visit to the Dalada Maligawa. Ever since the relic was brought to the island – wrapped in an Orissan princess's hair, they say – it had been a symbol of political sovereignty as well as a focus of

Above and right: *Castle Hill and the view across the great man-made lake to the town of Kandy – traditionally the centre of Sri Lankan culture.*

158

religious veneration. Soon after its arrival in Kandy in 1590, it was lodged in the great moated shrine built by the king. There pilgrims and tourists flock to see it, though what they see is only the gold-plated reliquary. The highly theatrical rituals around the viewing were impressive, but the enormous crowds prompted me to hurry away to dinner at Castle Hill. The British high commissioner had arrived and taken the other half of the house.

The next day was Independence Day, marking the anniversary of the relatively peaceful transfer of power from Whitehall to Colombo. But rather than stay to watch the processions and celebrations in Kandy, we drove to outlying Buddhist shrines in the morning and to the Botanical Gardens in the afternoon. Both were man-made, of course, but both were in beautiful natural settings: the fourteenth-century stone temples high on hills overlooking green fields, the gardens a feast of local and foreign flora. At the temples I noted the pungent smell of cloves and the wonderfully crafted paintings and carvings of swans, eagles, lions, lotus flowers, wrestlers, soldiers, dancing girls, musicians, and a mother suckling her infant child. At the gardens I noted that the holiday crowds and merry students were being watched closely by soldiers and police.

In the evening, though we had been cautioned against it, we went out for a

One of the Isurumuniya temple rock carvings, showing a travelling horseman at rest.

brief visit to Udawatta-Kele, a bird and game sanctuary set in a jungle of trop-ical trees. I had been there as a boy and wanted to feel its great peace. Recent-ly, however, it had been a scene of conflict, and more than three hundred JVP supporters had been found dead in the area. It was perhaps a stupid idea to visit there at dusk, particularly since it was too late to see any birds, but we encountered only a couple of armed guards who wondered what we were up to and turned us away.

Back at Castle Hill, as the swifts and swallows flitted unafraid through the open drawing-room that was rich with the fragrance of frangipani and bougainvillaea, I found it hard to grasp the violence and massacres that had plagued the pretty town below. But they were there, fresh in memory and lurk-ing in the approaching darkness.

In Kandy's market I had seen a small and colourful fish I vaguely recognized. I asked what it was. A scorpion fish. In some places it's a rare delicacy and is rumoured to give a psychological high if eaten in sufficient quantity. I've never tasted it, but I once caught one in the Florida Keys. Just as I was about to pull it free from the line, my guide yelled not to touch it. It has a protective venom, he said. If the venom penetrates the skin of your finger, you have to cut off the

Another Isurumuniya rock carving – of a baby elephant playing in a pool.

161

finger or you'll die within minutes. Like the island of Sri Lanka, I thought: such beauty, such a high, and so potentially lethal.

I had a vivid recollection of the long red road to Anuradhapura from the days when my father and I had taken it. Once we descended the hills from Kandy, the dusty track ran straight north a hundred miles to the fabulous ruins. Every now and then there was a clearing in the jungle with a village and people selling king coconuts, papaws, betel nuts, soft drinks, vegetables, rice, maize, and spices. In front of many houses was a sea of red and green chillies drying in the sun. We stopped only twice: once to admire the Aukana Buddha, a fifth-century statue rising over forty-two feet, the world's tallest standing Buddha; and once to visit the impressive cave temples at Dambulla, which date from the second century B.C. King Valagamba took refuge there after being driven from Anuradhapura and built a shrine in gratitude when he returned to power.

"All down the ages holy men have lived apart in grand, mysterious places out of the world," mused W.T. Keble, my headmaster at St. Thomas's prep school and author of the wonderful old guidebook I carried, *Ceylon Beaten Track*. "They have tried to turn the mysticism of their souls into forms of wood and stone, of words and paintings, so that common people might understand at least something of the splendid vision, and use it to guide their lives in the hot, restless world outside. There is mystery and awe in the deep caves of Dambulla: they were made to cover the hermit who could find no satisfaction in feeding the earthly desires that bound him to the endless wheel of rebirth, and who sought escape from an illogical, quarrelsome world into the peace of a great liberation, which he could find no words to express, except to call it a no-thingness, a cessation of desire."

Drier landscape, hotter weather. Hotter politics, too, for we had left the relative security of central Sri Lanka and were moving towards Tamil territory. Though the contested Tamil "border" began north of Anuradhapura, the villages through which we passed were still mostly Sinhalese. Even so, we were not far from where the infamous massacre of Buddhist pilgrims had occurred. Nor were the numerous Sri Lankan army checkpoints very reassuring. There was so much unrest in the area, so many factions fighting each other, so little information, that I began to feel even more uncomfortable than I had in Yala.

Chillies drying by the side of the road leading north to Anuradhapura.

We reached our goal by lunchtime, arriving parched and hungry at the Tissa Wewa rest house, an especially pleasant two-storey bungalow in a park-like setting beside a shaded tank. How delicious the fish curry. How quenching the cold beers. How soothing the electric fan. How happy the memories of when my father and I had been together here.

Despite all that, we charged off into the heat and dust to Mihintale, a rocky hill seven miles away. Here, in 307 B.C., King Devanampiyatissa was out hunting when he spied a great elk grazing in the forest. Unwilling to take the animal unawares, he sounded a warning and the elk fled. The king pursued it, and it led him to Mahinda, the famous Buddhist teacher sent to Ceylon from India by the Emperor Asoka. The monk called the king's name, the king put down his bow, and their encounter led to the establishment of Buddhism on the island. There is a shrine up 1,840 steps at the top of the hill. On our tour of the sacred ruins I counted more soldiers than pilgrims or tourists.

Long before the birth of Christ, while the Greek empire flourished and most other parts of the world were emerging from the late Stone Age, Sri Lanka was a great civilization. It had well-ordered cities, five major roads, a complex irrigation system, and major trading centres. But, because only Buddhist structures were considered worthy of stone, there is little to be seen of the civil kingdom. In its time, however, Anuradhapura was the greatest city of the empire, and its remains still display might to match the pyramids of Egypt and beauty to equal the delicacy of Athens. It had been built as a capital in the fourth century B.C. by King Pandukabhaya, who had come to power by defeating all ten of his uncles for the throne – thus fulfilling a prophecy that had caused his grandfather to imprison his mother in a futile attempt to prevent the slaying of her brothers by her unborn child. For 1,400 years, until the tenth century A.D., Anuradhapura was the capital of the island, and its influence spread from the Tiber to the Yellow Sea. The city itself covered twenty square miles, contained tens of thousands of people, had three-storey houses and thriving industries, and boasted a bejewelled palace of one thousand chambers and gold shrines.

For most of the eight hundred years after the capital was shifted to the more strategically situated Polonnaruwa, Anuradhapura was left to the arid jungle. Only the sacred Bo tree remained alive.

In the 1820s a young British civil servant rediscovered the ruins, though it took another fifty years to get much official interest and twenty more years to begin excavation. Eventually, however, the combination of Sinhalese nationalism

Anuradhapura, with the old Jethawana dagoba and the beautiful Ruwanveli Seya in the distance.

and Buddhist fervour created a new passion for the island's ancient heritage, and politics and pilgrimages restored honour to the site.

The night's oppressive heat made the mosquito netting unbearable, but the mosquitoes were too persistent to make me throw it off. Dawn came as a relief from a wretched sleep.

The morning newspaper carried the following item: "A father and his two sons were shot dead and their bodies burnt by unknown persons in Anuradhapura on Sunday, a government communiqué said." It was Tuesday, and the deaths had happened when the three of us were bathing in the tank a few yards from our rest house.

I felt more vulnerable because I had no local source of news, no early warning system like the one Shirley Perera and Edmund Wilson had provided in Yala. There were guns and rumours and threats wherever we went in Anuradhapura, there were stories of a brutal slaying of local JVP supporters three weeks before, but no one actually prevented us from driving or walking among the deserted monuments.

The monuments were splendid and powerful, as if the sun and heat were making them reverberate with force. There were huge steps leading to grand and open chambers and nine-storey palaces reduced to 1,600 columns. Massive dagobas – round, domed shrines – stood four hundred feet high and the same in diameter. There were towers, pools, pleasure gardens, temples, rock carvings of lovers wooing and elephants playing. The sacred Bo tree, the oldest historically documented tree in the world, was brought as a sapling from the tree under which the Buddha attained enlightenment in Buddha Gaya. It had been worshipped here for twenty-three centuries. Its ancient limbs were supported by iron crutches.

Mostly we were alone, with our guide for facts and our imaginations to embellish the facts with fantasies. Occasionally vendors approached to offer coconuts or fake relics, but they served only to excite my wonder at what their ancestors had built and what it had all been reduced to: rubble and legends. If I hadn't been wearing my safari hat, I might have worried that the sun and dust were making me mad with visions.

Near the ruins of the Brazen Palace was where Duttha Gamini, a great and

A woman bathing before sunset in the great Tissa Wewa in Anuradhapura.

devout king, had died. "Formerly I fought with you, the ten great warriors, by my side," he said to the company gathered around his deathbed. "Now I have entered alone upon the battle with death, and the foe death I cannot conquer."

To which the chief monk replied, "O Great King, fear not, ruler of men. Without conquering the foe sin, the foe death is unconquerable. All that has come into this transitory existence must necessarily perish also, perishable is all that exists; thus did the Master teach. Mortality overcomes even the Buddhas, untouched by shame or fear; therefore think thou: All that exists is perishable, full of sorrow, unreal. In thy last mortal existence thy love for the true doctrine was indeed great. Albeit the world of gods was within thy sight, yet didst thou, renouncing heavenly bliss, return to this world and didst many works of merit in manifold ways. Moreover, the setting up of sole sovereignty by thee did serve to bring glory to the doctrine. Oh thou who art rich in merit, think on all those works of merit accomplished by thee even to this present day, then will all be well with thee straightaway."

"In single combat also thou art my help," the king said.

Standing on this sacred spot and reading those words in W.T. Keble's book, I mused, as Keble had done, upon the remarkable king's life. "He had been Duttha Gamini, the naughty boy, who sent his father a woman's ornament because his father would not let him fight the Tamils; he had been prince Gamini whose insatiable ambition could not brook being hemmed in, and would not rest until the whole Island was under his sway; he was King Gamini who repented of the bloodshed and sorrow that his long wars had caused and who strove to wipe out their stain by refusing to overtax his people, by countless gifts and works of merit, and by the great buildings with which he adorned his capital. But now he is Gamini the man who on his deathbed longs for the old friends of his fighting days, who rejoices at the great works that he has carried out and yet feels how small they are compared to his acts of kindness when he was himself in trouble; who fears death and yet meets it with unfailing courage."

Late in the day we thought of driving the twenty-eight miles to the Wilpattu National Park, on the chance that it had been reopened since the dreadful massacre of 1985. The odds of getting into a corner of it were slight, however, and there were general reports that it was still a terrorist stronghold and hideout.

Two Buddhist nuns bringing offerings to the Ruwanveli Seya.

I passed a happy two hours before the light faded, looking at the birds on Anuradhapura's two enormous tanks and photographing the villagers who had come to bathe in the cool water and the evening glow. The tanks were spectacular achievements by the kings of the second and third centuries A.D., and they remain vital to the existence of the present town. Linked by magnificent canals and controlled by high dykes, they are really vast and scenic lakes stretching for miles into the distance and surrounded by trees and picturesque ruins. Perhaps at no other time on my journey home had I felt such magic and such peace as during those two hours, watching the birds, studying the village faces, savouring the composition of light and water. I had to drag myself away reluctantly. It was getting dark, and the dark was not safe.

The dark also conjured up images of the romantic past, specifically of the year 1679. Night had just fallen when two men, fugitives from the government, crept out of the hollow tree in which they had been hiding not far from Tissa Wewa. They were almost naked, heavily bearded, and badly sunburned. The men were two British sailors named Robert Knox and Stephen Rutland, and they had recently escaped from Kandy, where they had been held captive by King Rajasinha II for twenty years. Disguised as poor pedlars, they had reached Anuradhapura on their way to freedom in the north. They had encountered wild animals, soldiers, savage tribes, and hunger, and more trouble lay ahead. They survived, however, and made it back to England the next year. There Robert Knox wrote an account of his adventures in his *Historical Relation of the Island of Ceylon*, and some of them were borrowed by his friend, Daniel Defoe, for a book called *Robinson Crusoe*.

It was only fifty miles to Sigiriya, and we reached it by noon. The first sight of the massive red rock rising six hundred feet above the green scrubland against the clear blue sky took my breath away. The impression was as overpowering as it must have been fifteen centuries ago, when the rock fortress contained one of the loveliest cities ever to have graced the earth.

"For millions of years this grim giant stood above the jungle before the coming of man; for a million years its rugged sides defied man's climbing feet. In due time for a brief moment, the flood-light of history lit it with a blaze of

Sigiriya, the dramatic rock fortress chosen by the mad genius Kasyapa in the fifth century as the site for his royal seat.

glory, and then moved on, and left the ancient fortress as a lonely landmark for the dwellers of the jungle," I read in my Keble. "It must have been a twisted city of steps and stairways and quaint buildings perched on rocky pinnacles, and strange caves hidden under boulders – a quaint, elfin city, innocent of straight lines, and following the lie of the land without any assistance from geometry, like a city of a fairy tale."

Inscriptions on boulders confirm that Sigiriya was a retreat for Buddhist monks at a very early date. In the fifth century, it was chosen as the site for a royal seat by Kasyapa, a mad genius operating under a paranoiac fear. The oldest son of King Dhatusena, who built the tanks at Anuradhapura, Kasyapa developed an obsession that he would lose the throne to his younger half-brother. As a result, he overthrew his father, imprisoned him, and demanded all his wealth. Dhatusena led him to a view of water in his greatest irrigation system. "There," the old king said, raising water in his cupped hands, "this is all the treasure that I possess." Outraged, Kasyapa ordered his father's death, and the old man was walled alive within a tomb.

Fear, arrogance, and a delusion of divinity then drove Kasyapa to construct his palace atop the dramatic rock at Sigiriya. It took seven years to build, and he stayed there eleven years, secure within its impregnability, until lured out to engage his brother's army on the plains below. At the height of the battle, apparently, his elephant turned away from a hidden swamp, and his army mistook the move as a sign of retreat, leaving Kasyapa alone and defenceless. Flamboyant to the last, he drew his dagger, cut his own throat, raised the blade high in the air, and returned it to its sheath before falling dead.

On the western outskirts of the modern town at the base of the fortress were several villages that had once been full of JVP supporters. Six weeks before, they had been massacred. We saw many abandoned huts and few young men. The women, children, and old people who remained were being harassed by wild elephants, which had moved into the newly deserted compounds and taken advantage of the absence of strong defenders. I took some photographs of the remarkably well-dressed and happy school children and of the elderly survivors – many of whom had attained a great age, probably because of their diet of fruit and vegetables.

Despite vandalism and the passage of almost 1,500 years, a few of the five hundred beautiful frescos of the Sigiriya maidens have survived.

We climbed the long and steep staircase and walked past the symmetrical ponds of the old water gardens into what had been the main palace. We were awed by the remains of throne halls and audience chambers, but even their splendour paled in comparison when we came to the incredible frescos of the Sigiriya maidens – and the famous graffiti dedicated over the centuries to their praises. Once there were five hundred of these sensuous beauties on the gleaming walls, but monks and vandals had obliterated all but eighteen. It was hard to imagine that these masterpieces had been lost in the jungle for hundreds of years until rediscovered by an incredulous British hunter in the middle of the nineteenth century.

As happened when I was a boy, because of all the hornets I couldn't climb to the very summit, up the steep steps carved between the clawed paws and menacing jaws of a giant stone lion.

The small rest house was much the same as when my father and I had stayed there, though more run-down, busier, and beside a paved road instead of a dirt track. It wasn't as comfortable as the two new hotels built largely for Western tourists, but I preferred it for nostalgic reasons. In the evening I photographed

Sensual images of dwarfs around the exotic Demalamahaseya temple in Polonnaruwa.

174

some birds in the overgrown grounds and noted again one theory about the name of the rock that towered overhead. Traditionally, Sigiriya is supposed to originate from the words for lion and throat, but I couldn't see any lion's throat except for the one carved near the summit. On the other hand, from a point below the western entrance, the rock's silhouette always looked to me like the profile of a giant male lion. There shouldn't be any doubt, therefore, that the name means Lion Rock and was bestowed on the natural formation long before Kasyapa made the lion the symbol of his mighty fortress.

The lion is the symbol of Sri Lanka. The tiger is the symbol of the Tamil rebels. The leopard, which sometimes shares the name of the tiger, is plentiful here and known to kill humans. Lions, tigers, leopards, rebels, they filled my head that night, and I associated them with the wayside robbers who used to ambush travellers heading north on the old track past Sigiriya when I had been here as a boy. And speaking of ambush, I was attacked mercilessly by an end-less army of mosquitoes. The overhead fan helped drive some of them off, but its whirring noise hid the footsteps of armed men and wild beasts.

Tomorrow, I thought, into Punanai at last.

Polonnaruwa was only thirty-five miles to the east. A large morning cloud hovered over the lion's head like a grey crown as we drove away from Sigiriya, farther into Tiger territory.

Compared to Anuradhapura, Polonnaruwa had a brief and uncomplicated history: two centuries of glory and twelve kings. By the sixth century A.D. it had been a military camp of some importance as a crossing of the Mahaweli River. After the Cholas invaded and conquered Anuradhapura in the eleventh century, the capital was moved to Polonnaruwa; and though the Cholas were soon defeated again by the Sinhalese, the Sinhalese King Vijayabahu did not move the throne back to Anuradhapura. The kingdom prospered despite continual invasions from India and Malaya, but late in the thirteenth century the capital was moved to the west, and Polonnaruwa was lost to the jungle until the British began their excavations.

The rest house where we breakfasted was beside the "inland sea" created as the city's irrigation source – which it still is – by King Parakramabahu I, King Vijayabahu's grandson. We soon dashed away to see the ruins of palaces, baths, temples, defences, and residences. We visited caves containing inscriptions from the second century B.C. and monastic chambers showing traces of the brilliant murals that once decorated them; and then we stood in awe of the three giant statues of the Buddha carved out of rock, standing, reclining, and in meditation.

My mind wasn't totally focused on what I was seeing, I must admit. We were extremely hot and tired, the tour seemed rushed, and there was a tightness in my stomach; I wanted to get on to Punanai.

Getting to Punanai had become necessary, an obsession, though it was another forty miles deeper into Tamil Tiger country. I knew it was dangerous to go there, but I was more afraid of not finishing what I had set out to do than of the risks of the journey. The place had come to symbolize so much for me – a sort of psychic and emotional Everest. I had no reason to believe there would be anything dramatic to "see," but I needed to experience whatever was there to be experienced. Not to be able to go would leave me feeling as if my trip had been an empty exercise.

At noon, sitting on the veranda of the rest house overlooking the vast lake, I told Raja that I wanted to go right away, even if I had to travel alone. Again I

The Kirivehera dagoba in Polonnaruwa dates from the eleventh century.
Overleaf: The glorious Gal Vihara in Polonnaruwa – one of the most spectacular rock carvings in the ancient city.

was told about the dangers: the road lay through guerrilla-infested jungle, the Tigers were in control of the area after taking it from the Indian peace-keeping troops and keeping it from the Sri Lankan army, and neither the Tigers nor the army were keen to have strangers going in. We had a long and intense discussion about the trip. Raja was worried, but he wouldn't let me go by myself. Although he was Sinhalese he was relatively dark, and he spoke Tamil. He had even been as far as Batticaloa and Trincomalee and back, so he felt fairly safe. Childers and Lucky looked clearly Sinhalese, he warned, and I could be mistaken for a foreign correspondent, so the threat of ambush or instant killing was real. If I had to go, he concluded, it would be better to go without the other two and without seeming too eager for information and photographs.

Why did I feel in my bones that Punanai would be my own final destination? I was certain I was going to be killed, and though I didn't say it, I felt guilty for involving Raja in a perhaps foolhardy undertaking. We looked at each other for a long time in silence. The sense of crisis was like the heat and humidity that build up before the monsoon breaks. Then I went to find Childers and Lucky in their rooms. I agreed with Raja that it would be crazy to bring them along, but I felt I had to tell them of our plans and let them decide their own movements.

Over lunch I announced that Raja and I were leaving afterwards for Punanai and I explained my hurry. Tensions seemed to be mounting in the region, I said, and I wanted to go while the going was possible. Raja then went over the political and military situation in Sinhalese. There was a moment's hesitation when he finished, then Lucky said, "Listen, Chris. We've come all this way with you. We might as well finish with you. Besides, we want to be in on the kill too!"

We laughed and the tension was broken. There was nothing more to be said. So we stood up and shook hands all around. I could hardly wait for our rice and curry to arrive, so that we could finish quickly and be gone. We ate in silence. It was hot and the mosquitoes were a menace. Thank God for the electric fan, I thought. It makes life a little more bearable.

We took few possessions, in case we were accosted: only one camera and no knives. We packed water, fruit, and chocolate, in case we were left stranded somewhere. Then we piled into Raja's car and headed northeast, out of town, and on

Over the course of only two years in the early 1920s an exceptionally audacious leopard killed and devoured at least twenty human beings in the region of Punanai, keeping the tiny village in terror.

to the long and empty road – the same road on which travellers and villagers had lost their lives to the dreaded man-eater more than half a century before.

At noon on May 22, 1924, Captain R. Shelton Agar received a telegram from the Government Agent, Eastern Province, Ceylon. "Reward Rs. 100/- offered destruction man-eating leopard Punanai ten miles from Valachenai* ferry," it stated.

Captain Agar hardly needed one hundred rupees. He was a prosperous estate owner and tea planter in the Hatton district, with long family connections to the colony. But the offer made him "quite excited," as he wrote later, because he had never heard of such a leopard before. He had shot leopard at a water-hole, he had watched a leopard kill, he had stumbled upon leopards in the jungle, he had killed rogue elephants and other mad beasts, but the idea of going after a clever cat with a taste for human flesh struck him as an "interesting undertaking."

"Starting immediately arrange local trackers to meet me and guide me to the place," he wired back at once, and by midnight he was on his way. Badulla by three. Maha Oya by six. Valachenai by nine. A two-hour wait for the ferry. At last, within a day of receiving the telegram, but not for an eternity according to his impatience, he reached the place where the leopard had pounced upon its latest victim three days earlier. All that remained was a head cloth hanging on some bushes and a large pool of blood by the roadside. Captain Agar examined the evidence carefully and concluded "that a terrific fight for life must have taken place here."

Despite his "keen desire" to find the spot where the leopard had dined, he chose to wait for the arrival of the "expert jungle men" he had summoned to help. In the meantime, he plotted his strategies: to patrol the road day and night, to set out goats as bait, to use local hunters and their dogs, or even to make a trap with human bait inside. In the afternoon he forsook an opportunity to kill a huge elephant he encountered, because it was doing no harm. "The mere shooting on sight and slaying in the jungle is not sport," he stated. "The real joy of the jungle is the following up and killing of dangerous and mischievous beasts, the collecting of rare and beautiful specimens, and the study of the growth and habits of animal and wild life of the jungle – that is sport of a most extraordinarily absorbing nature."

At six in the evening he began his night patrol in a blaze of flashlights and acetylene lamps. Nothing. Towards midnight he rested for three hours, then began his early-morning patrol. Shortly after three he saw a family of leopards on the road.

There are two accounts of the man-eater of Punanai, one by Captain Agar, one by railway inspector A.H. Altendorff. In basing my own narrative on their stories I have retained the spelling "Valachenai" for today's Valaichchenai.

The male, female, and one cub sprang away quickly, but Captain Agar had a moment to fire from his car at the second cub. He missed. Soon afterwards, however, the first cub reappeared. Captain Agar got it with both barrels of his Paradox. Then he managed to wound the second cub in its right hind leg before it fled back into the thicket. He did wonder if the head of this family was the monster, driven by the lack of sufficient game to prey on humans, but he didn't believe so, and later events proved him right.

His patrols continued the next day and night, and again he saw the male and female around four in the morning. This time the female leapt suddenly at his car. The captain shot and missed, but his driver's bullet caught the leopard in the stomach. One more to kill, the captain noted.

Early the following day he met eight men returning to their homes near Batticaloa from the tobacco fields.

Travellers were a rare sight, and the man-eater was their only topic of conversation, but these eight felt safe enough because of their numbers and their arsenal of weapons (including swords, knives, axes, and a gun). They boasted to the captain of how they were afraid of nothing, especially not of the fierce man-eater. Such was their boast that Captain Agar decided to play a prank when he came upon them a second time from behind. Talking loudly and staring intently into the jungle, they didn't hear his car approach slowly to within yards of their backs. Then he had his driver honk the horn.

"Pandemonium reigned," Agar reported. "There were yells and screams. Axes, swords, and knives were thrown to the winds. They were paralysed with fright thinking it was the man-eater. Had it been him, he could have dealt with the lot."

Back at his camp he found that the trackers had arrived with the sacrificial goat, which bleated incessantly, exactly what Agar wanted from his bait. "Nothing happened on patrol that night," he observed, anxious for the next day's goat stunt, "except that my car was chased by an elephant."

Early in the morning the captain and the trackers followed the bloody trail of the man-eater's most recent victim. They found a matchbox, a twenty-five-cent piece, some tobacco, a waist cloth, a hairy scalp, then a dreadful stench, and finally a terrible sight: a body without a head; mauled legs and scratched arms. But no signs that a leopard had been there recently. Studying the evidence, the captain pieced together the fatal scene. A quick and sudden attack. The tall man seized by the throat and dragged between the leopard's four legs. "It made one's blood boil to think of such ferocity and created a determination in me, at whatever risk, to try and rid the place of such a pest."

But, he suddenly wondered, was the mad beast crouching even now behind a stump or waiting on a branch, observing everything, knowing everything, ready to spring?

"I realized with a shock I would be the hunted, not the hunter this time. All my movements would be closely watched by a hidden foe whose attack would be launched at any moment from anywhere, front or behind, right or left, or above. I must be prepared somehow or other to defend myself."

He surveyed his weapons: a long-range duck gun, a 416-bore magazine, a D.B. 470 express, a 600-bore rifle. All were lethal, but of what use in an unexpected charge? He had more confidence in his knife in a tight fight for life than in his old friends the big bores. But then an inspiration struck him. There at the bottom of the ammunition case was his 450 automatic cordite pistol, "the man stopper," shining and loaded! "It was no sooner thought of than I had it out and slipped under my belt ready for instant use," he declared, "and with it my confidence returned."

It wasn't needed, however. "The goat stunt was an absolute failure. The hitherto noisy creature was absolutely mute in the jungle and shivered with fright. Nothing we could do would raise a 'Ba' out of him."

Despondent, impatient, the captain soon gave up. For the moment, at least.

There wasn't much conversation in our car, though our shared sense of risk seemed to bring the four of us closer together. We saw hardly anyone. Just arid scrub and tall grass. Perfect ambush country, I thought, for leopards or for men.

Two army checkpoints detained us for questioning immediately to the west of Punanai.

Then, quite suddenly, Childers spoke to Raja in Sinhalese. Raja nodded his head, as if agreeing to let Childers tell me the same thing in English. They had learned before leaving Polonnaruwa that the situation in this area had deteriorated recently. The Tigers had replaced the Indian troops, but no one knew when, where, or what it meant. It was too late for me to turn around, however.

Immediately to the west of Punanai we were stopped by two armed soldiers at a Sri Lankan army checkpoint. They took Lucky and Raja into a hut for questioning. Where were they going? For what purpose? Didn't they realize the danger? Did they have any weapons? Were they smuggling in food or valuables? Who was the foreigner? Was he a reporter? Why did he want to write a book about a man-eating leopard of almost seventy years ago?

They detained us for about ten minutes, and though they thought I was crazy, they let us proceed. But don't stay too long, they warned, and don't get out of the car too often.

Almost immediately, however, we ran into a second army checkpoint – or so the guards claimed, though I had to wonder if it wasn't really a Tiger checkpoint in disguise. More of the same questions, more of the same bewilderment. A book about a dead leopard? Okay, we could pass, but we weren't to talk to anyone in Punanai about the political situation or report on it when we left.

So we drove into the village. Punanai! Punanai!

In 1924 A.H. Altendorff was working in Punanai as an inspector for the construction of the railway extension between Batticaloa and Trincomalee. On the morning of August 16 he gave his mail to his servant, Manickam, and ordered him to take it to the Kalkudah office along the old road. Altendorff specified "the old road" because he had been hearing for more than a year about the monster leopard that had eaten nineteen people to date at a particular point on the main road. He had even received a first-hand account from one of his workmen, whose friend had been killed as they walked together through the jungle. The leopard had sprung from the tall grass beside the road and leapt on the back of his horrified prey.

About an hour after Manickam left, Altendorff learned from his cook during breakfast that his servant had disobeyed and gone by the shorter main road. Panicked, the railway inspector rushed out and sped off on his motorcycle. The road was straight, and before long he could see Manickam walking about a mile in the distance, towards the leopard's killing place. It was too late, however, because suddenly the servant vanished. When Altendorff reached the site, there were only a bag, a head cloth, signs of a struggle, and a wide mark that showed where a body had been dragged into the jungle.

Altendorff raced ahead to where forty labourers were clearing the grass from the side of the road, as part of the inspector's efforts to reduce the risk to his frightened workers. He chose four of the bravest, who were armed with knives and axes, and led them back to cut a trail following the leopard's bloody path. But they refused. It was too dangerous. The leopard was near, hiding, furiously protecting his meal.

"My anxiety was great to find out whether it was possible even at that stage to save my peon," Altendorff recounted later. "I therefore set to clearing the scrub myself, but I suppose there is, at a time like this, some protective force for which we cannot give a reasonable explanation, which compelled me to stop clearing and I retreated to the road with my four men."

Feeling his life had been spared by a moment, he dashed on to Kalkudah for help. Mr. Samuels, the engineer, gave him a note for Mr. Matthews, the executive engineer, and Mr. Matthews gave him a telegram to send to the government agent in Batticaloa. By coincidence Captain Shelton Agar, the noted sportsman, was with the government agent there, and almost at once a telegram came back to Mr. Matthews: Captain Agar was on his way.

The captain was clearly delighted to have another bash at the man-eating leopard. He had more or less given up on the idea, until fate (in the form of a frustrated hunt for a rogue elephant) brought him to Batticaloa just as the news of the servant's death arrived. A "great chance," Captain Agar enthused, because the kill had been so recent. "In the ordinary course of events," the captain noted, "the information would have been given to a Headman, who would have probably pulled his whiskers for a day or so, thinking the matter over before passing it on to another Headman above him, and he in turn would stroke his beard for another day or so before passing the information on to headquarters. So the news often arrives too late for any prospect of success."

At two on Sunday afternoon, August 17, the captain met the inspector ("nice, pleasant-spoken," thought Agar) at the Valachenai ferry – "men ready, no delays, everything nicely laid on" – and they hurried on to the fatal spot at Mile 28, only a few yards from where Captain Agar had been the previous May. By four o'clock they were moving cautiously into the bush in single file: a labourer clearing the trail, the captain, another labourer, the captain's driver, another labourer, the inspector, and the fourth labourer at the rear. Captain Agar gave firm instructions that the first shot would be his.

Twenty feet in, they heard the buzz of thousands of bluebottles. A little farther on, they found Manickam's clothes and cigarettes, as well as the skull of another victim. Then the servant's nude body, terribly bitten at the neck and propped up against a pallu tree.

"All the insides and a good part of the left leg had been eaten," the captain observed. "The face, arms, and right leg had not been touched. The body was fairly fresh. I felt certain we had disturbed the leopard at his feed and that he was lurking nearby."

The captain ordered an ambush to be built in a tree. His plan was to wait, day and night, for the leopard to return to eat. As the four labourers worked on the platform, the others stood guard. The tension was so great that, when they suddenly heard a growl twenty feet away, Captain Agar's cigarette dropped from his lips! "Shoot and shoot to kill!" the captain yelled. But nothing came.

Meanwhile, a drizzle had started, the light was fading, and the group had neither lanterns nor flashlights. So everyone opted to return to Punanai to fetch them and some dinner. Before doing so, the captain got the workers to tie the corpse by its toe to a tree, so that the leopard couldn't drag it away. Terror hung over their retreat. "In a few seconds the feeling of imminent danger increased so intensely," Altendorff remembered, "that I was forced to look back and lo and behold! About 40 ft. away was the man-eater, in full view, heading for us!! A magnificent but terrifying sight!"

Accounts differ as to what happened next – an understandable confusion, given the circumstances. Either Altendorff got off a shot and missed, or the captain's driver screamed, "Leopard, Sir!" However alerted, Captain Agar saw a glimpse of yellow near the corpse and banged off two shots. One of them seemed to be a hit, but the man-eater was able to disappear again. "It all happened in a flash," the captain recorded. "This daring beast had been watching us the whole afternoon, and now had come to take away the kill he thought we had left." This time he ordered the workers to tie up the corpse by its legs.

When they returned after eight in the blackness of the night jungle, however, they were startled to discover that the body was gone.

"We have no luck with this leopard," the captain said to his driver.

"No, Sir, but we had better get off quick."

The reply knocked Captain Agar to his senses, he admitted later. "I realised what a mad, foolish and dangerous thing I was doing. In these exciting moments I had thrown all caution to the winds – approaching a man-eating leopard's kill on a dark night, with only torch light to guide us, and exposing my people and myself to danger! What was the leopard doing now? That he had hidden his kill safely away was obvious. The question was, 'Was he coming to look after us?' I ordered a quick retreat."

Yelling at the top of their lungs, enough to scare the leopard and "all the devils in the jungle," they fled. "Needless to say," Altendorff wrote, "our exit from the jungle broke all records of speed. We got into the car and drove off to Punanai for the night." There the captain refused both food and a comfortable bed. He fumed most of the night in the car, "too 'fed up' for words."

Like Agar, I too realized what a mad, foolish, and dangerous thing I was doing. In these exciting moments I had thrown all caution to the winds – but there was no quick retreat.

For Agar and Altendorff this small village of Punanai represented safety from the leopard. For me it was the night jungle. The threat was there, unseen, wounded, angry, ready to pounce. The Tamil rebels' flag – a tiger's head emblazoned against crossed guns on an orange background – flew in the breeze above the main roadside house, which had belonged to the station-master until taken over by the Indian troops and then the Tigers. The newness of the flagpole, really just two thin and freshly cut bamboo sticks, showed how temporary and recent the occupation was. However, we saw no cadres.

At the edge of the road there was a stall offering ginger tea. Raja got out and talked to some villagers at it. Explanatory gestures, questioning looks, fingers and eyes aimed at us in the car, more questions. Then Raja waved for us to come. I couldn't help noticing the guns lying in the grass nearby.

By six the next morning Captain Agar and his company were back in the jungle. They followed the track of the corpse – the mark of a toe being dragged across the wet ground – and soon found the skull stripped of its flesh. Then they heard the crunching of bones in the thicket. They moved towards the noises, guns ready, the captain now "desperate" for a kill. "There!" cried a tracker, pointing. "There!" cried another, pointing somewhere else. "Shoot! Shoot!" cried a third, pointing to a patch of brown. But it was only a sambur. The leopard had fled.

"Suddenly we saw the corpse!" the captain wrote. "Evidently the crunching sound we had heard had been caused by the leopard feeding off the ribs. I vowed that I would not let that body out of my sight again day or night, until the end came one way or the other. My spirits, which sunk to zero in the evening, now began to come back again."

Again Agar ordered an ambush to be built within sight of the body. The platform and seat were completed by eleven o'clock, and the corpse was pulled into the clearing seven feet below. A sambur called in alarm, as if the man-eater were near and watching. The body, swarming with flies, stank.

"What about human brains vs. feline cunning?" the captain asked himself, and he decided to try a trick. He had his trackers walk away loudly, as they had the night before, in the hope that the leopard would return to his feast. Captain Agar and his driver waited on the ambush as the voices faded away, but the leopard never

A hazardous reminder: the Tamil rebels' flag – a tiger's head emblazoned against crossed guns on an orange background – flies above the main roadside house in Punanai.

came. "He apparently had no use for this brain wave stuff," the captain concluded, and the trackers were summoned back.

Everyone took position on the platform or in the trees, waited, waited, and waited. Silent in a silence disturbed only by mosquitoes. Two hours passed. By early afternoon the men became hungry and thirsty, and they realized they had better bring supplies for a long night. Captain Agar sent all the others away on the expedition. He would remain alone at the watch, true to his vow never to leave the corpse.

"Do you mind being left alone?" his driver asked.

"Of course not," the captain replied. But as soon as they departed, he began to feel loneliness and fear.

He wrote: "I began to think of serious matters, for danger was very near, indeed. The alarm call of the sambur made that clear. A cable I received a few weeks ago came vividly before my mind: 'Very anxious please stop hunting leopard.' I had not listened to that plea from far away. Someone was thinking of me. I realised that all my faculties would have to be extended to their utmost. I missed at once the little scraps of whispered conversation I had been having with somebody close by. My own pair of eyes had now to do the work that four pairs of eyes had been doing; they had to keep a constant and sharp look-out everywhere. My nerves were strained to their very limits and my imagination was also playing tricks with me. The thud caused by the fall of a rotten branch made me swing round and draw a bead in that direction. The creaking of one tree against another fixed my attention, and the sudden sharp noises of birds, etc., sounds that I would have instantly recognised and placed in the ordinary way, made me start. I misinterpreted the ever-changing play of light on the fallen leaves. Near a mound, in a shadow, I saw leopard colours which gave me concern. The picture altered with the sun. My position now was not the comfortable one I had arranged for myself. Instead, I was standing up in the middle of this platform of thin vibrating sticks, with rifle ready for immediate use, trying to keep a look-out everywhere. There was only one way for the leopard to gain his kill again, and that was past my rifle. He would have to do for me first. I was expecting an attack any moment. I ask you, reader, a question. Have you ever experienced the sensation of icy water trickling slowly down your back? The cold shivers! A sudden weakness of the knee joints!! A quivering of the legs!!! It comes suddenly at certain psychological moments, and is caused by such circumstances as intense excitement, anticipation, fear, etc. I had no fear of the leopard. I was there to meet him. Seeing red, so to say. I knew the business would be short and sweet either way. Put yourself, reader, for a moment in my place. Alone in the jungle! An unrecognisable mass of decomposing human flesh that only a day ago was an able-bodied man, close by, and now emitting a dreadful

The station-master at Punanai.

191

odour, and attracting an ever-increasing multitude of buzzing flies, and a demon in the shape of a man-eating leopard lurking somewhere near, waiting for his chance. This is the naked picture for you, but there was always God above."

At the tea stall Raja talked in Tamil with the villagers – some of them Tamil Tigers – while Childers, Lucky, and I sipped the hot and sweet ginger drink in silence. Better than the taste was the excuse it gave me to do something with my nervous hands. I didn't know the language and felt out of place, but the people seemed friendly enough, though curious and amazed when I took a photograph. I hoped Childers and Lucky wouldn't begin speaking Sinhalese to each other.

We ordered a second cup, and Raja and I sat at the edge of the road with two young Punanai men. Had they ever heard of the man-eating leopard or Shelton Agar? Raja asked for me. No, they were too young, of course, and the story was too old. Instead, they began to talk about the Tigers.

"They are near, very near," I was told. "They come at night."

"Does that scare you?"

"No, it makes us feel safe. We are happy to have them here. They saved us from the Indian soldiers. They protect us. The Indians scared us. They used to torture us, even our women and small boys."

Altendorff returned with the trackers, equipment, and a bottle of tea for Captain Agar by three o'clock after enduring two terrifying treks through the jungle under the spell of the powerful and fearless man-eater. "I stood idle on the ambush, thrown to the wind with God above," the captain informed him when they met again on the platform. (Or so the railway inspector claimed. Agar's reminiscence put only himself and his driver on the ambush just before the glory came.)

Everyone was back in place and quiet once more. Rain fell, soaking them thoroughly. Captain Agar drank his tea. Then the leopard appeared. In Altendorff's version, Mangar, the driver, had heard a leaf rustling, had looked and seen the man-eater near the kill, had nudged the captain – who had dropped his tea. In Agar's version the captain himself had glimpsed the leopard's white stomach during a casual glance over his left shoulder. In both versions, however, the leopard was staring up at the platform, baring its fangs, swishing its tail – as Agar put it, "just like some beautiful white devil."

As we sat in the afternoon sun a train pulled into the Punanai station on its way to Batticaloa, and visions of A.H. Altendorff danced in my head. Suddenly I felt very bold, almost giddy, and I got Lucky to accompany me across the bridge over the railway tracks and down to the station platform. This was the sort of situation we had been warned to avoid. We were exposed in a public place, surrounded by hundreds of unknown people coming and going beside the train. Even so, I felt oddly invulnerable.

I began taking scores of photographs of faces and the colourful scene. I had Lucky take a picture of me standing under the "Punanai" sign and the Tiger flag; and we tracked down the station-master, a small man with a wide grey moustache, to ask him if anyone remembered the man-eater.

"There were many leopards here when I was a boy," he said. "My father always warned me how dangerous they were. But I haven't heard of a leopard for years. I suppose they're all dead."

"What about the man-eater? Did you hear about it when you were a boy? Does anyone here speak of when Captain Agar came and shot it?"

The station-master thought for a moment and shook his head. "It happened so long ago. There are not many old people in this village. Death comes early here, and it comes here often. And why remember old evils? So many evils have come to Punanai since then, it's better not to think about them all. Why bother with an old leopard? We have enough to worry about now."

"You mean, the Tigers."

"They don't worry me too much, though they took over my house last week as their headquarters." He smiled broadly. "They don't hurt us. But be careful. You are strangers here. They will be back at dusk. If I were you, I would leave soon. I don't think you'll find anything about leopards here. They've all been killed."

We shook hands, I took his photograph, and Lucky and I walked away. We hadn't gone far, however, before the station-master rushed up. "Wait! I've just thought of someone. There's an old man near here, he's sort of an uncle of mine. I'll get a boy to take you to him. Maybe he can answer your questions."

While waiting for the boy, I sent Lucky back to the tea stall to fetch Raja. I was going to need a Tamil translator with me. When he arrived, we were guided through the crowd and beyond the station to a mud hut down a sandy path. The old man was lying on a string bed in the shade, chewing betel nut with only a few teeth. He must have been nearly ninety. He was very feeble, his eyes were glazed with grey cataracts, and his wispy hair hung over a face ravaged by time. He seemed worried at first, as if we were government agents, but then he was merely puzzled. Yes, he remembered the man-eater. Yes, he remembered hearing of Agar. But that was all: there had been a leopard that killed many people until it was killed by the Englishman. No, he couldn't recall any more details. No, he didn't know of any other villager who could help me.

I was disappointed, of course. It seemed so anticlimactic. We sat in silence for a while, the old man spat some red stain on the ground, and I got ready to go. Then he said:

"It wasn't just a leopard. It was the she-devil, the *divi dos*, Kuveni's curse."

"Kuveni was the queen of the Yakkas, who seduced Vijaya, the founder of this island," Raja reminded me after he had translated. "Their children became the Veddas, the primitive tribe who still live in this region." Then he turned back to the old man. "What about Kuveni?"

"She was angry, very angry, when Vijaya banished her and married the beautiful princess," he said. "She wanted to kill him. She became a leopard and tried to go into his bedroom. But Vijaya was protected by his guards. Then Kuveni stuck out a long tongue, a tongue made of crystal, to curse him with its touch. A soldier cut off the tongue and put it in a golden box, but it was too late. The tongue became a leopard again, and when the box was opened it fled into the night. The king never recovered from the curse and died with no children. That is the *divi dos*, the evil of the she-devil."

"And it lived in the man-eater?" I asked.

"It lived after Vijaya's death," he replied. "It haunted the next ruler, King Panduvasdeva, too. He had to bring his people from Malabar to cure the spell with dances and charms. They keep those dances and charms in Kandy, but Kandy is far away. We had no magic to fight the *divi dos* until the Englishman brought the dances from Kandy. He did the dances in the jungle. He performed the rituals with offerings of food. He chanted the verses to command the evil to leave us. He was a great man, as great as the King of Malabar. There are leopards now but they don't bother us."

After half an hour we heard the train pulling away with two sharp whistles. I gave the old man some money, and Raja and I hurried back to the station after agreeing to keep the unusual legend to ourselves. The crowds had dispersed quickly, and there was relative peace and emptiness around the station. The train was just a speck in the distance, an overcrowded memory moving north into dangerous country. Dangerous country now, dangerous country when Agar and Altendorff were here, but different dangers. We rejoined Childers, who had been very concerned by our lengthy absence. We had another cup of ginger tea, but I hardly needed it. My adrenalin was running high, and I felt punchy with our daring. I was standing above a clearing amid a jungle of terrorists. I was taking aim at my man-eating obsession. And there it appeared, like some beautiful white devil, baring its fangs, swishing its tail – my father's self-destructive madness within me!

Captain Shelton Agar slipped off the safety catch of his D.B. 470 express and slowly raised the gun. "I knew at that range I could place the bullet where I liked, and I chose the neck shot, as I knew at that angle the explosive bullet would rake the creature's vital organs. At the shot the leopard rolled over – stone dead – never to do any more dirty work."

Everyone cheered with pleasure and relief, and the people of Punanai turned out to celebrate as the hated beast was carried on a stout pole and then by car into town. The lusty and jubilant rejoicing went on and on, reward enough for Captain Agar – besides, of course, a whisky and soda at the railway superintendent's bungalow and a chance to get away as quickly as possible from the cursed place with its ugly sights and putrid smells in the jungle. "I wanted some vast, wonderful, sweet-smelling perfume to come all over me," he remembered later, but he had to be content with the knowledge that his task was done.

I walked up and down the main road of Punanai alone. It was probably a stupid gesture, but I felt absolutely safe. For weeks I had gone around Sri Lanka with a sense of dread. Something tragic always seemed just around the corner or hard on my heels. The adrenalin was pumping into my bloodstream the whole time; I rarely slept well; I felt pursued by bad tidings and wretched ghosts. I got used to it, to an extent; it became as much a part of my life as it was for the people of the island, but it wouldn't give me peace. Then, when I entered directly into the atmosphere of doom – here, where the threat was most real – my fear suddenly turned inexplicably into euphoria, punchiness, a feeling of invulnerability. I calmly took a photograph of a smiling villager holding up the two fish he had just caught. Death may have been very close to each of us, but we shared a moment of joy. We were totally alive and marvellously happy, he with his fish, I with my photograph.

In dramatic terms I should have died at that moment, been killed perhaps by a knife entering suddenly into my flesh. Maybe that's why I had come to Punanai, after all. Certainly I wouldn't have regretted such a perfect death. But fate had other intentions for me, it seemed, and led me home.

Even in that moment of emotional release, however, fear gave a last flick of the whip. A young man came over to us. "They're here already," he whispered, gesturing towards the ground. "They're hiding in tunnels under this road. They can hear everything, but no one can see them. They know you're here, and they don't like it."

Lucky, Childers, and Raja looked nervous and pleaded with me to retreat back to Polonnaruwa before dark. Perhaps to their surprise, I made no objection. I had done what I wanted to do. Now I could pay attention to the voice of caution. So we got into the car and drove off, each lost in his own silence, each at the end of his own journey, each savouring his own small triumph over the devil that drives.

6

Epilogue

Back in Colombo, on the eve of my fifty-seventh birthday a few days later, I went to the Colombo museum to see the man-eater of Punanai, stuffed and donated by Captain Shelton Agar. Past the magnificent Kandyan jewellery, past the unique statue of Tara, past the portrait of the last queen of Kandy, and there it was: a female, I was certain, not a male, smaller and narrower than I had imagined, about six feet long, captured forever, and utterly harmless. What terror this sorry-looking exhibit had once inspired!

Outside, on the streets of the capital, a new terror had taken hold. Richard de Zoysa, a prominent and popular journalist and broadcaster, had been abducted from his mother's house in Nawala, only a few hundred yards from Gillian's, and found murdered two days later. He was only thirty-five years old, and though his death was just one of many while I was on the island, it sent waves of fear and rumour through the city.

Death had also taken two of the three people whom I had been counting on for details about the man-eater and about Captain Agar. Even in Punanai, as I had discovered, there weren't many people alive with personal memories of those events in the 1920s, so each loss seemed a tragedy. The first was Arul, the slain tracker who was supposed to take me into Punanai. The second was Sam Kadirgamar, the ageing lawyer and wildlife enthusiast who had been such a close friend of my uncle Noel. He had told Gillian that I should telephone him as soon as I arrived in Sri Lanka, that he had some crucial information for me, but when I tried to contact him, I was told he was extremely ill with kidney

Dr. Hamish Sproule told me more than I had bargained for. Did the man-eater of Punanai carry a curse too?
Previous page: North of Colombo, coastal outrigger canoes in the evening sunlight.

problems. Later, he was taken to hospital in India, and then when I got back to Colombo from Punanai, I was told he had died there.

That left only Hamish Sproule, Michael Sproule's father and Gillian's former guardian. I couldn't help thinking about the death of Shelley Crozier's three friends by the "curse of the devil bird." Did the man-eater of Punanai carry a curse too?

Naturally I was impatient to see Hamish, and by chance I had the perfect excuse to visit him right away. Soon after getting back to Colombo, I developed a high fever with long shivering spells – sure signs of malaria, which had been rampant in the Anuradhapura area. Hamish, besides being a great friend to my family, was a retired doctor, so I went to see him at Holmlea, the marvellous old colonial house once owned by the de Sarams and the Colombo centre of all our childhood activities. Much of the land around the house had been sold off, but the great house still maintained a glorious presence, and on entering it I felt I was stepping back into the past.

"Odd you should ask about Agar," he said, after he had given me some advice about the fever. We had settled down to tea. "I first met him when he came to Dr. Spittel's nursing home, also to be treated for a bout of malaria. Everybody seemed to have it in those days."

The same Dr. Spittel who wrote about the notorious devil bird. A double coincidence, I thought.

"In fact, Chris, you really remind me of Agar in other ways. Same age, same height, same physique, same confidence, same fire in the eye, and apparently the same obsession with the Punanai leopard! He had already shot it by then, of course, he was even famous for it, but I never found him a braggart. There was much fuss made about him in the papers, but he simply went back to his tea estate up in the Hatton district. He was quite a humble man, but he loved a challenge and loved the outdoors. Besides being a great sportsman, you know, he was a very successful planter. His family had long connections with Ceylon. Even after Shelton's retirement in England, he used to come back for visits. He

The crudely stuffed and mounted body of the notorious Punanai leopard was donated by Captain Shelton Agar to the Colombo museum.

loved the place. It got into his blood, I guess. It always does. You understand this now. People come, people go. But they always seem to come back."

"But it *is* my blood," I protested.

"Of course, of course, but you have been away so long, you have so few connections here now, that I wonder why anyone would return to this tragic place. For it is tragic, you realize. But I suppose there is a magic too. We had so much, we have so much, yet we have torn down our past and torn ourselves apart. You must see the change even more than I do. In many ways your father was lucky not to live to see all this destruction. I believe he could see it coming, and he just didn't know how to live in this new era. I remember talking about it some time after he left Kuttapitiya. He seemed really down then, and totally confused about the situation."

"I wouldn't have described him as lucky in his last years," I said, "but you're probably right about his inability to adapt. He always seemed to me from another age, a more golden age, that never prepared him for the real world."

"All of us in that set were pampered, it's true, but Mervyn was special. We adored him, of course, for his fun and liveliness. He could get away with murder, and often did. But we all knew that there was a dark side to his character. His wildness could be extreme, and it bordered on self-destruction even then. But you have to understand him as we, his friends, did. His father was both indulgent and demanding, rather a formidable figure, and Mervyn felt both protected and inadequate. That's a dangerous combination in a young man. It makes you feel superior, beyond the normal bounds of behaviour, while it also makes you feel inferior, causing you to lash out at the world and hurt even those whom you love most."

"Certainly he lashed out at us sometimes," I said, "but I never imagined it came from an inferiority complex. His anger always scared us. It was unpredictable, but in the end he always seemed to be right. He was a very demanding father."

Hamish laughed. "My God, Chris, you make poor Mervyn sound like the man-eater himself! He wasn't like that at all. I may not know all that you children saw, of course, but children really are their parents' worst judges. Gillian used to speak of him in the same way when she was a girl with us. But we always tried to make her remember his best qualities. He loved you all so much, you know. He often told me that his family was the most precious thing in his life."

"Then why on earth did he destroy it?"

"I don't know. Why did he destroy himself? Why is this country destroying itself? In fact, why is mankind destroying this planet? There are no simple answers to these questions. Mervyn was just a human being, with all the complexity and darkness that suggests. We all have to get past our questions and our grievances. All I can say is, whatever it is you have been searching for, whatever it is you have been hunting – like Agar and his leopard – you must learn to accept your father as a mere man and not some evil god."

"That would be a lot easier," I answered, "if he hadn't left us with such a feeling of guilt and shame. It has taken me forty years to come back here because of it."

"Now you remind me much more of your father than of Agar," Hamish said, "with all this talk of shame. He never forgave himself for losing his family and position, and it seems that you haven't really forgiven him either. You must be careful that you don't inherit his anger and bitterness too. Of course he made mistakes and behaved rather badly to everyone, particularly your mother. We all saw that. But, as I told him on several occasions, we never disowned him or hated him. He was family, part of us, and most of us accepted him in bad times as well as good. In fact, I would say, we accepted him more than he accepted himself, because we loved him more than he loved himself. You should try to do the same."

Hamish Sproule was silent for a while and then spoke very softly. "I'm going to tell you something, though maybe I shouldn't. Your father was ruined by debt, and I have always wondered why. He wasn't a big spender. He worked very hard. Most of his reckless days were behind him. True, your mother could be extravagant, but your father wasn't particularly so. After all, drinking doesn't cost that much, and Mervyn didn't gamble. So why did he have to borrow? My guess is that he borrowed heavily to send you to England and to pay for your school fees! These are things you've quite obviously used to incredible advantage. Without those expenses, however, it seems to me, he might have survived. I don't want to be harsh about this, but his ruin might have come from his love for you."

I left Hamish's house feeling both moved and confused. My father *had* been a gambler, but not at the tables or the track. Instead he had gambled on me. If he saw me now, would he think it had been worth it?

I needed some time alone, to write out my notes and think about what Hamish had said. So I phoned Gillian and told her I would be out for dinner, and I went to the Galle Face Hotel.

The Galle Face Hotel still symbolizes the colonial era in Colombo. It's a magnificent palace by the ocean, with palm trees in the lobby, waiters wearing elaborate uniforms, fans whirring on the ceilings, and an aura of genteel society. It seemed particularly seductive at night, and I was glad I had dressed up before going to Hamish's.

The Galle Face had been my father's home away from home in Colombo, and I remembered being here on one of the last occasions I was with my mother and father together. The three of us had gone to dinner in the Royal Dining

Room – probably Ceylon's most exclusive dining-room at the time and a watering hole for many wealthy planters and civil servants. It was a hot night but the fans weren't working, so my father took off his jacket and draped it over the back of his chair. The waiter came over and asked him to put it back on – jackets were mandatory in the dining-room – but my father refused. Then a second waiter came over to make the same request, and again my father refused. Finally the very austere headwaiter came over and said, "I'm sorry, sir, but if you don't put on your jacket, you will have to leave." My father got up, grabbed his coat from the back of the chair, and stormed off. I was left in silence with my mother. Once more we had been deeply and publicly embarrassed by my father's behaviour, and I knew that my mother was worried about what trouble he would get up to next.

This incident, though small in itself, came back to me vividly as I sat in the Royal Dining Room. I even experienced the hot sensation of embarrassment again.

It was odd, I thought. Ostensibly I had returned to Sri Lanka to learn about the man-eater of Punanai. That had led me unexpectedly into the heart of terrorist activity. But everywhere I went, my father's ghost kept reappearing – with the leopards at Yala as well as on his tea estate, with the Tigers in Punanai as well as at Rock Hill. More than that, I began to realize that my whole life may have been haunted by my father's ghost. It had followed me – driven me – from England to Canada, from hardship to wealth, and back once more to the island where I had been born.

The more I thought about it, the more it seemed as if the entire history of this island was a variation on the theme of fathers battling sons. In the Vedda legend about the devil bird, the father murdered his son. In the story of Vijaya, the son was banished by his father and went off to found a kingdom of his own. Hadn't Duttha Gamini rebelled against his father, and hadn't Kasyapa caused his own father's death?

Even today the efforts of the Sri Lankan government to put down the Tamil Tigers and the JVP seem another expression of paternal authority against the revolt of the sons. The lesson seemed clear, like a universal law of nature: if you don't come to terms with the ghost of your father, it will never let you be your own man.

It may have been wishful thinking, but I felt that Hamish had helped me face my father's ghost at last. Certainly I was seized by a sudden sense of happiness. In a gesture that may have seemed mad to the others in the Royal Dining Room of the Galle Face Hotel, I stood up, took off my jacket, and draped it over the back of my chair.